Venier Voldo, A. L. Bancroft

**Poems From The Pacific**

The West's Reply To England's Laureate

Venier Voldo, A. L. Bancroft

**Poems From The Pacific**

*The West's Reply To England's Laureate*

ISBN/EAN: 9783744652155

Printed in Europe, USA, Canada, Australia, Japan

Cover: Foto ©ninafisch / pixelio.de

More available books at **www.hansebooks.com**

# POEMS FROM THE PACIFIC

THE WEST'S REPLY TO ENGLAND'S LAUREATE

BY

## VENIER VOLDO

AUTHOR OF "A SONG OF AMERICA" AND MINOR LYRICS

SECOND EDITION.

SAN FRANCISCO
THE BANCROFT COMPANY
1888

TO
CLARA FOLTZ

THE PORTIA OF THE PACIFIC

Who, filling many niches in the Pantheon of Life, has adorned
them all with a lofty womanhood

THIS VOLUME IS ADMIRINGLY INSCRIBED

BY

THE AUTHOR

# CONTENTS

| | PAGE |
|---|---|
| DEDICATION | 3 |
| PREFACE | 7 |
| MY LORD THE LAUREATE | 9 |

SPENCERIAN IMPRESSIONS.
| | | |
|---|---|---|
| I. | Ave Parnassides | 21 |
| II. | Sun and Storm in the Coast Range | 22 |
| III. | Poesis | 23 |
| IV. | Shoshone Falls | 23 |
| V. | Pacific | 24 |
| VI. | Religio Naturalis | 25 |
| VII. | Youth and Ambition | 26 |
| VIII. | "O, Woman's Eyes" | 27 |

SONNETS.
| | | |
|---|---|---|
| I. | Sappho | 29 |
| II. | Byron | 30 |
| III. | Lincoln | 30 |
| IV. | Woman | 31 |
| V. | Freedom | 31 |
| VI. | To Anne | 32 |
| VII. | To Festus | 32 |
| VIII. | Night | 33 |

SONGS AND BALLADS.
| | |
|---|---|
| "How Brightly on the Laughing River" | 37 |
| For an Album | 38 |
| "If a Man Stand Up to the Storm Like a Man" | 38 |
| "Swift May the Tune of Spring" | 39 |
| Psalm of Courage | 40 |
| "O, Whence the Delight of Thy Face" | 42 |
| Mignon | 43 |
| "Thy Wrongs Have Made Thee Sacred" | 44 |
| Love's Omnipresence | 45 |
| "Sweet Memories of Other Days" | 46 |
| "O, With a Light Heart and a Merry" | 47 |
| Ma Belle | 48 |
| "Not All the Strings that Thrill with Fire" | 49 |
| My Love's the Life | 50 |

## CONTENTS

**PAGE**

SONGS AND BALLADS.—(*Continued.*)
Thine Eyes .................................................................. 51
"You Have Said the Charmed Words" ............................. 52
"O, Hope Lift Up Thy Weary Wings" ............................. 53
"Fain Would I Tell" ........................................................ 54
"Call Not The Promise Vain" ......................................... 55
"Let Us Be Conscious How Happy We Are" .................... 56
Look up, Poor Heart ....................................................... 56
"Fine Was His Voice Whose Ruddy Lip" ........................ 57
"If Dreams Have Tongues" ............................................. 59
"Cease Thy Tremulous Plaint" ....................................... 59

MISCELLANEOUS.
Sierra's Good-Night to the Sun God ............................... 63
Clara Foltz, Jurist—Mother—Woman ............................. 66
Hymn to the Calm Night ................................................ 67
Good-speed to Men ........................................................ 71
Yolonde with the Yellow Hair ........................................ 72
The Ministry of Nature .................................................. 75
Birth-song of Aphrodite ................................................. 78
Seven Sisters .................................................................. 81
"Ah, For The Day That Has No Voice" .......................... 85
Juliette ........................................................................... 86
"I Saw Thee and I Loved Thee" ..................................... 87
The Comedy of Evil ....................................................... 89
Aphroditis—A Passion Monody ..................................... 91
The Muse Humanity ...................................................... 97
Venus Urania ................................................................. 98
In Memoriam—Henry Wadsworth Longfellow ............... 101
The Changes of the Shell ............................................... 105
Ode to Columbia ........................................................... 109
A Lament for Childe Harold .......................................... 117
Thy Naked Feet ............................................................. 124
The Garden of the Sea—A Revery on the Birth of California ... 126
Gloria Militaire .............................................................. 130
"Come!" ......................................................................... 132
Memoria in Eterna ......................................................... 133
Walt Whitman ............................................................... 136
For Woman's Sake ......................................................... 139
"Through the Rays Serene" ........................................... 140
Shasta ............................................................................ 141
Contemplation on the Uxmal Ruins ............................... 142
The Wasting of the Flowers .......................................... 144
"Where Rolls the Oregon" ............................................. 149
Yosemite ........................................................................ 151
Lyric of Labor—Upharsin is Writ on the Wall! .............. 152

A TRINODY.
Abelard and Heloise ...................................................... 155
Antony and Cleopatra .................................................... 157
Paola and Francesca ...................................................... 159
"The Birth of Song" ...................................................... 165

# PREFACE.

The writing of such a poem as the second Locksley Hall, is something more than a literary blunder; it is a sin against civilization. There were limits, it would seem, to the unprogressive dotage of even octogenarianhood; but the conservative cynicism of Carlyle and Tennyson proves that "reversion" may sometimes, indeed, "drag evolution in the mud." What muffled adieus are these as contrasted with the sublime farewells of Sophocles, Simonides, Chaucer, Goethe, and Longfellow?

In the work before us the author condemns a world he refuses to understand. The mighty facts that breathe and burn about us touch not a muse whose loftiest flight insults the spirit of the age. The light-bringers of the century bear no torch for him. Science is busy only with the new astronomy, which discovers the moon to be dead, but not with home-building for the living millions of the earth, nor with the new chemistry of human happiness. "Poor old history" finds good not in the present, where it is, but in the past, where it is not. The poet's later vision is all too narrow to perceive the glorious indices which are making history grander than itself; philanthropy, with love's lamp searching out the haunts of the wretched; legislation, seeking to be humane and just, protecting the weak, enlightening the dark, uplifting the oppressed; politics, exalting and expanding civilization; letters, reaching after hope, and strength, and joy; science, discovering the unity and completion of the race.

But not for the poet-peer to "live into a gentler time." For him no "suffrage of the plow," no "federation of the world." He forgets that social problems have always vexed, but that a brave age will solve them bravely. He perceives not that the present is a protest against "petrified old forms, tyranny, and the devil;" and that out of its seething and agitation new forms will arise into larger liberty, higher achievement, supremer happiness.

The age, true enough, discovers shameful defaults, and man improves too slowly for his aspirations. But our laureate spends his force in idle lamenting, vain regret, wasteful blame. He denies remedy, libels liberty, denounces equal rights, debilitates courage, ignores the forward movement of the nations, discourages the onward hope of the world.

What has the race done to my Lord the Laureate, who like Seneca writes about poverty on tables of gold, and who with never a sorrow of his own, might better employ his muse in solacing and strengthening the world, rather than in deepening its shadows? The writer of these fragmentary lines—written in wide apart interludes of duty and always beneath the pall of torturesome care—might with far more consistency pose as a pessimist. Such a luckless Wandering Jew to whom life has denied even the privilege of finding out whether he could write verses or not, has earned some right to condemn the world and riot in its hopelessness. But how does such an one, deeply lettered in the iron alphabet of experience, find more to praise than to blame in the black earth, more to inspire a pæan than a lamentation? Life is largely what we make of it; and there is one cowardice to look back from the plow, and one heroism to look up and on. Verily, the world moves despite its laureates; and he who will not help it on with a word of brave cheer is its enemy and not its friend.

THE AUTHOR.

# MY LORD THE LAUREATE

### SIXTY YEARS AFTER

Cold upon the silent Cellyne creep the leaden hours along,
Dead the Nestor of the ancient, dead the singer, and the song.

Hath the old no dying courage, shall its doing be undone?
Dead to-night, re-born to-morrow; deathless glory of the sun!

O, deathless man; the dust is quick here where mighty Hermes lay;
Resigned the sceptre of December to the magic wand of May.

O, golden Nestor, say what word may still the babble of your boy?
Learn you of olden folly, child, of the folly of old Troy.

When Heaven and earth, when Gods and men, invoked the seas and skies,
And a world's glory rose and set within a woman's eyes.

The boyhood of the new has come; lo, the old had boyhood too;
Both plod in gloom of the vile and false for pearls of the good and true.

Both in life's troubled ethics versed would evolve the higher man,
Awed by the wealth of mystery in the Planner and the Plan:

The one wild tale of life in death, of joy out of wreck and rack,
Great Hector plunged in the hell of war from the heaven of Andromache.

The one fierce tale of coming man, coming but never yet come:
Dumb at the first as beast or bird, and to-day but the lesser dumb.

Crude at the first as slime of sea ere she bore on her whited breast,
The gift of Woman, the gift of Power and gift of Love's unrest.

Yea, come you hither, boy indeed; your love was a shrew and cheat:
How far have you been undone in the base Olympia of deceit?

Her sister, you knew, had wed a churl, and unwed without a sigh,
Two fools conspired with wise old Time to woo and marry a lie!

And you? well, life hath its cross, alas, tho' yours is no deep sea rage;
You have survived to be later lost in the chaff-heaps of the age.

And your curse is not a weightier thing than e'en your worldling's laugh:
The age is greedy enough, but has no monopoly of chaff.

For once was there irony of joy in Babylonia's hall,
Riot was writ on the hearts of men and Upharsin on the wall.

For once a Lord of Laughter lived; the Aristophanic ryme,
Who sung of "Birds" and "Clouds" and "Wasps" and "Vanities" of his time.

Then the comic anger Plautus roared and the slave Terentius raved,
The Ambubabæs hymns of hell that the lash of Lucian braved.

The chaff of Eternal Rome, alas, and the purple Cæsar's strife,
Lo, Juvenal and his furious scorn of their games of "dice" and life!

Apicius, drunk on wine of pearls drained to the very lees,
Paulina in her jeweled dress of forty million sesterces!

O, age of gorgeous criminals whose lips at their great slaves curled,
When royal robbers rode unmasked through the highways of the world.

O, vain dead froth of human ways, O, frailty base and bare,
Or whence Cervantes biting wit, or contempt of fierce Voltaire?

So in each throbbing round of Time since the sage began as boy,
Lovers are false and fools are mad and mystery is a toy!

And wizard man is small and great and marriage is great and small,
The ages swing 'twixt love and hate for the hope that passeth all.

For the hope and miracle of light that beams from Beauty's face,
And health and strength and mighty joy and majesty of the race.

O, hush not the Forward! Forward! 't is the cry of life to be,
What death is there whose voices ring from thy grave, O Thermopylæ?

The Knighthood of the world is sought and the manhood of the slave,
The conquest of despair and death and victory of the grave!

In truth a cruel yesterday: great Egypt graveward flings
Her children's hapless bones up-piled as monuments to her kings.

And cold the shuddering wings of night, the barbarian's sunless swarth;
The roses of the West adorn the skeleton of the North!

And thou, O royal beast, O Rome; behold your gladiators slay;
Self butchery of valiant men to make your whelps a holiday!

The air is hushed and hope is still, and still the christian martyrs there;
Red the arena's ghastly sands—it is only a savage lair!

And lo, Siberia's spectre grim, the Cremara's purple snout,
The Swine-kings reign by grace of God and heraldry of the knout!

Yea, read the wide world's annals well, illumined with blood and gall,
Where Chaos is king and Woe is man, while Crime holds carnival.

Yea, old Experience is wise because a fool the day before;
Creeds, superstitions, arms, have each accursed men with their score.

No more the wisdom of the past than its folly is our friend;
What not to do the legacy exalting an endless end.

Break! break! indeed, the olden State, dead church and barren throne!
Their echoes shudder adown the years, dead echo of a groan!

And "roll their ruins down the slope;" the ashes of night and rage,
Time has found his goldenest fruit, an emancipated age.

"Poor old History!" Tale of Sorrow! States undone 'twixt Dis and Mars;
But for Greed "the globe we groan in" might be fairest of all stars.

"Poor old Heraldry;" empty glamour! blindly leading blinded men!
Old political lack of sense forever mocks the might have been!

Whilom sang a youthful singer, neither Lord nor Laureate;
Silver and rose life's morning time, and golden its last estate.

Silver of faith and gold of hope, voice of the coming not the gone;
"The glad earth should not stand agaze like Joshua's moon at Ajalon."

But talk a tiptoe with the stars enamored of the beck'ning view,
Science with her magic lamps and fairy mansions of the new.

Lit by the happy eyes of love, O, swift the hero history ran,
The oracles of space declared the sovereign destiny of man.

High his meridian of fame, then backward bent his fair renown,
The regal singer of a race, the herald only of a crown.

The little boasts of what has been hush the prophetic great to be,
The old Throne sets its craft to rhyme emblazoned in weird royalty.

And vacant pageants of the Past pose shimmering in idle trance,
The Roco-Cupid scorn of fact the folly-fever of Romance.

Wan Melancholy's empty wail, powdered wiggery and Watteau,
Strength create to build and bless a-waste in emptiness of woe.

Thus doubtingly with sombre strings the Poet sang unto the sage;
The doleful aftertone of harps imprisoned in the middle age.

Sang of the dust of Chivalry and mediæval dust of pride,
The splendors of the feudal day but not the shame of which it died.

The Golden Ass Apuleius and dizzy pleasures that he clomb,
Not of the wronged plebeian mob, the naked Nineveh of Rome.

Of garters, crests and golden mail, ribboned scarf and falcon lore,
When men like birds of bonnet fame were known by plumages they wore.

Tame bells of jesting odalisques, a satin and patchouly line,
Adopti having charmed of fate a special charter to be fine.

Soft echoes of the good old time when lofty barons for a show
Coined laughter out of human want and minstrelsy of human woe.

Such was the alphabet of air, Elvish sheen and cruel tears,
By which the singing courtier learned the argument of mighty years.

Such the "Hail Cæsar" of a muse attuned in an immortal school;
The weak shall kiss their plunderers, the robbers of mankind shall rule;

And take no "suffrage of the plow;" what wills have these except to yield?
Annointed heirs of stolen power hear not "the voices from the field!"

Enough for these when danger threats to gather from their busy hives,
And save their country with their blood, and shield their princess with their lives.

Is this your "wholesome old world dust" before the newer shall begin?
"Noises of a current narrowing:" Yours is the lawless din!

War and blood those fancy most who have no drop of blood to give;
Half a million minions perish that a useless prince may live.

Nay, not from gray thoughts such as these shall men arise with lofty cheer;
The Prophet bowed to gilded dust, the poet fallen to the peer.

Lo! here reversion! here Death's song, the long disease of selfish blood.
Here the falsehood "ever dragging Evolution in the mud;"

When great poets sing small themes, then indeed the angels weep;
Ghosts of fickle dreams that slumber, ghosts of promises that sleep.

Chaos Cosmos! Hasten backward! Vice is clammoring in the street,
The higher age perceives it clearer, therefore let us sound retreat!

Zola pois'ning maiden fancies, boyhood feeding from the sewer,
Never age so crammed with madness and the leprosies that lure.

Why, then, sing a fiftieth matin glorying your sovereign's name?
Rather chant a lamentation or a vesper hymn of shame!

Peace! Peace! O poet, lame and old, passing on into the night,
The lamp of your ideal youth would give your lame feet better light.

Before that fatal passion's fire sweeping through had left you dry,
"Left you with a palsied heart and left you with a jaundiced eye."

Before the couriers of the mind searched out the old dead lie of things,
To gild the praise of feudal crime and the apology of kings.

Before your hope winged with the morn and faith with olive leaves un-
furled,
Had lost their Eden for mankind, their hallelujah for the world.

When with joyance bounding upward you embraced the newer day;
"Better fifty years of Europe than a cycle of Cathay!"

Chaos Cosmos! Downward beckon! let the iron hearted earth,
Reach its man-subliming summit, ranging backward to its birth!

O, graceless vain philosphy of spent and of outrun years!
Stay not the winged soul! feast not on husks of wars and fears!

O Peace! chill minstrelsy of self; hymns of "I" and "my" and "mine,"
Sing now the kinship of the "our" and the harmony of the Nine!

The universal, dazzling dream! Fraternity at Cosmic feast!
Accursed the polity that bears the future symbols of the beast!

Marks of the dragon of the pit! loud bellowing for Self and Self!
Not rights for all that suffer wrong, but rights for Ghibbeline or Guelph.

Poet, Statesman, teacher, friend, O heed ye that divinest call,
Comradeship for every being, "all for each and each for all."

Why chant ye of outspent forces of dead Shem and Ham and Seth,
What a great man failed in doing sixty winters after death?

Shades of Sophocles and Goethe! must a muse at eighty sing
Gladliest of a boy that babbles, and Narcissus at the spring?

And to-day! hath she not smallness! Yea, and shame and bitter wrong
What mortal curses crouch and blend through her comedy of song?

The Sepoy mocked the age's boast and died at the cannon's mouth;
Infernally re-echo still the crumbling chains of the south.

There are sons of toil for whose poor sakes the gold sun hardly shines,
Maimed and wasted and worn away at their cattle work in mines.

But the century is shocked and shamed at sight of waste and crime,
And scorn of men for a monster born is the measure of our time.

And hatefulness of the blind mad beast is less in the wide world's store
But fire of the living jewel of love is a sparkle more and more.

And less and less is the black night's dark and more is the red of day,
Kindlier, juster and nobler now the van that leads the way.

Stars have risen and set, but the light of the freed mind is our star,
Lincoln, Gladstone and Emerson, Renan and Castelar!

Pilots not of purple twilight, heralds of the rising sun!
For Truth shall yet be uppermost and justice shall yet be done!

And Forward! Forward! cry aloud! for the People's age has come,
The noble discontent of men refusing to be dumb!

Kings once owned the State and its joy was a royal jest and fling;
The Kingdom of Right has come to reign, the people now own the King!

And my Lord is equal with his kind, if my Lord be as tried and true:
The rank of man emblazons the shield of the good he dares to do.

Kings of Honor! these are Kings! this the first kingdom of earth's sands;
Yea, verily, earth's proper Lords are the "Lords of their own hands."

And woe for our Medean asps and our ingrate Regan worms,
But the Cosmic womb fails never a day with her diviner germs

And sweet Cordelia's bloom for us with perfume of nun-like love,
Spartan mothers bear heroes still, the strength and the fire thereof.

There were sounds of breaking of slave chains amid war's rumbling chant,
The sea forth gave its Farragut and the shore gave forth its Grant.

So hold not the Onward Present, " fatal daughter of the Past,"
Evolution! not Reversion! Man the victory at last!

Rehearse the Muse of Yesterday and inspire illustrious deeds,
But let no maxim voice for man the measure of his needs.

The feathered heels of Mercury are a snail's pace with his shell,
Beside the fire of Edison and the flash of Morse and Bell.

Freedom that is Progress, Selah! let the lustral soul inquire!
Science clear the field for Music! Lift the poet-vision higher!

Fuse with what is truly Hellenic, fired with high creative power,
Moulding states to light and beauty, lead them to their loftiest hour.

Through the dust of dying races an eternal sequence runs;
Conjures silent Life new changes for the conquest of the suns.

You have gazed on great Orion sloping slowly to the west!
'Tis the track of Aryan glory to the crown of Aryan rest.

Not the twilight West of Apap nor St. Brandon's shadowy isle,
Where Sun-heroes quench their glory in a greater than a Nile.

Across the path of desert sea or ghostly Acheron of seas
Shine in paradisal sunset groves of the Hesperides.

Not the dead's home, but the living's; else re-born the Orient dead,
Freed Odysseus bounding Sunward from the Hades that he fled.

Zone of Earth's supremest power and Thought's most luminous estate,
Forward from the Yellow Sea, and Sunward to the Golden Gate.

War has sung its grand Iliads, gone the Aryan voice of Greece,
And the westward race is listening for the Odysseys of peace.

Feudal pomp has piped its story, lords and kings and popes are sung;
Mother of Life, now sing of Freedom! the Immortal, ever young!

Sing of Freedom! Sing of Forward! Lo! a braver race is born
With song and sight and summer—golden monarchy of Morn!

Sing emancipated Woman! let not Justice stop at sex!
O. eternal Sphinx! what marvel that your riddles mock and vex!

When the dual Mind of races, male and female, blend in one,
Then and only will thought triumph crowned with halo of the sun!

Then and only codes be wisest and the people glad and great,
When all gifts of mind are garnered to the glory of the State.

When the mind and heart are wedded, when the Statesman and the Sage
Comrade with great souled Aspasias, then begins the Golden Age!

When the people's kingdoms flourish and not when republics fall,
Will men find their high ideals " all for each and each for all."

Unity of man! Life's marriage! Sovereignty to build and bind;
Not Indo-European oneness, but the oneness of mankind!

O, fate compelling Hope! O, Friend, that would not have release,
O, Love, balm-bringer unto man, sweet Olive of his peace,

What couriers of heaven are these that comforteth high and low,
Sweet healers of man's wretched health, swift winged in search of woe.

What emperors of Earth are those by nature royal born,
Far listening with gentle ears for the cry of those that mourn.

The Earth is but an infancy! and man its later marvel-joy.
Babe of a very babe is he—to-morrow will he be boy!

And one day man, indeed, and lord of Life's democracy of law,
In rhythmic balance with all things, star-browed and calm with awe.

And tame leviathan shall list and sea's finny beasts obey,
Boreas pause stone still to hear what the new god hath to say,

And the New Chemistry shall come, all quick with Cosmic breath,
To unlock and warm the icy North and cool the tropics of Death,

Reclaim the deserts of the earth with intense, life-giving throes,
Robbed nature's wastes make green again and blossom as the rose.

Age of fair Science and sweet calm! Image-breaking age of Sense!
Light and Leader come at last to herald Love's omnipotence!

O, door of the uplifted Muse! Science! Teacher! Key of Life!
Release the diadems of Strength from out the crucible of strife.

Finder thou of Life's good mother, fount and breath of human good,
Wake our universal kinship, warm our universal blood.

With gravity's slight silken chains link the endless worlds of space,
And man with every rhyme of all the ages of his race.

Cast out the curse of tyranny and cruel greed's alloy,
Let all men see the Cosmic sun and feel the Cosmic joy.

Lift up the sweat-gemmed brow of toil and arouse endeavor's pride,
The whole earth should man's Eden be, and Beauty all men's Bride.

And with kind hands unite true hearts and inspire where heroes fail,
Twine laurel of the Apennine with parsley of the Vale.

The noblest of us all is he who finds deepest wounds to bind:
Not latest Lord of Locksley Hall but latest lover of his kind.

# Spencerian Impressions

## I

## AVE PARNASSIDES

Hail burning breath of genius and of wit!
The radiant electricity of thought!
As Deity had will'd and Fire had writ,
And Beauty, Joy and Excellence had taught. .
Where is the fountain that my life has sought?
Castalius, pour thy youth of waters wide,
Thy balm with Spring's eternity so fraught,
Now, quaff and woo this everlasting Bride,
And gray renew thy gold as if't had never died.


All hail! O Spirit of the magic chord!
Lend of thy fire one spark to thrill my string,
My untried lyre gave by Apollo lord:
Hap'ly and oft in fancy journeying
Have I approached thy evangelic spring,
O proud Parnassus, and from the luscious bowl
Drank with a frenzied thirst, sighing to sing—
Come then, glad Nine, ye minstrels of the soul,
Awake each waiting pulse and let your numbers roll.

## II

## SUN AND STORM IN THE COAST RANGE

Fair Morning broke with an exultant joy,
And Nature put her purplest livery on;
The less'ning stars did with the sunbeams toy,
And glad the Earth as in his fulness shone
The Gold-king of the Day; it was the dawn
Of life as well as light—intensest life—
For birds and beasts and brooks did pleasure don,
Summit and vale with vocal glees were rife,
And 'mid such gracious stars, what thought of storm or strife?


Short ends the tune of Nature's lusty lyre!
And the bold blood crowds hard the swelling veins;
For see! anon! fierce clouds are sheathed in fire,
And the quick blaze reveals the weeping plains,
And the mount's havoc as the stern oak strains
Before the blast or grapples with the sod:
And Mars has given Jove the battle's reins. .
For such a war would have a parent god
To bid the awful flash and rule of rattling rod.


Lo, the Skies talk! and Ocean answers back
As each were angered with the other's threat
And would disbattle 'neath his passion's rack. .
And scared Space shudders as two worlds had met.
Each bent to prove itself most passionate,
And hot pursued, pursuing with hot rage,
Outpours the flood of its envenomed debt. .
Grasp! grasp! the story of this fearful page
When Diety and Dust their mighty powers engage!

## III

## POESIS

Sweet Poesy! thy glad gifts come to me,
So winged with heavenly freightage and refined,
So laden with enchanting mystery,
Quick with the royalties that burn and bind,
Awaking wondrous ecstacies of mind,
That I embrace thee with a frantic zeal,
Letting each wound of life thy rich balm find,
Or when distractions o'er my bosom steal,
Turn to thy nectrous spring and not in vain appeal.

## IV

## SHOSHONE FALLS*

Pause ye apace, for lo, what power is this—
What ocean spills her waters from her lap,
And casts them howling o'er yon dark abyss?
Now strain the eye, arrest the blood's smooth nap.
Impelling grandeur doth essay to wrap
The Soul of God within this awful curl,
And fill with majesty the springing gap.
Deep throes and terrors unremitting whirl,
And main and mist alike their gracious gifts unfurl.

And speech is hushed within its humble home,
Pride is rebuked and poor Self chastened here. .
Behold a world wherein the Soul may roam,
Flying its clay for an exhaustless cheer,

---
*These falls are fittingly described as the Niagara of the West.

Yet feasting with a reverential fear
At the All-Being's overwhelming board,
Where perfect goodness holds it wide career,
And life is sinewed in the roaring Word
Whose long and loud appeals are felt while they are heard.

And white Earth trembles 'neath the mighty tread,
Nor dares oppose the monster's headlong way,
Nor mock his groaning voices deep as dread,
Nor parallel his most sublime array. .
For his is a commanding, resolute sway,
That orders homage and obedient love
In the strong thunder of his glory's fray,
And while he wills the sternest will to move,
Asserts th' Repose of Power that Power alone can prove.

## V.

## PACIFIC

There is a pleasing terror in the sea,
A wild enchantment in its infinite waste,
There is a rapture in its roaring glee,
One language, one, that man has not defaced. .
The luscious land by fertile greenery traced
Has more of nutriment and gentle sweets,
But here where elements by fear are chased
The soul is moved, and shrinks from what it greets,
And roams in reverent awe these curling, liquid streets.

It is enough—here find a sacred height—
A watery Babel—where the soul may rise

With true ambition to the Source of light.
But when man lords thee, Sea, and vainly tries
To rule thee, thou dost yield his seeming prize,
Then breakest down the barriers of sense
With thy stern, cold negation, and the skies
Of Pride, or mockest at such poor defense,
Rebuking with thy Dreadfulness! Omnipotence!

## VI

## RELIGIO NATURALIS

Each fragile leaf, bud, flower, tells a tale
That not in all the creeds of Time is found!
Where is the bigot who will dare assail!
Love, Cleanliness, Obedience—the round
Of blessed means—and above all is crowned
The Joy of all, thanksgiving on each tongue,
That swells Creation's glorious resound,
As there were volumes in each tiny lung
Leaping to pour their floods of praises deep and young.


In truth's name ponder boldly—he is mad
Who does enslave the free estate of thought,
Letting the have be but the might have had..
Earth, space, all life is with religion fraught,
And sacraments of light not truly taught
By blind interpreters—grasp it and fill
As *thou* dost hunger for what is rightly sought,
Shall all be found, and shall supremely still
The else unanswered wish and unobedient will.

Give, give the soul its wing! 'T will reach a height,
That must needs shame the body's littleness,
And lead it to the mountain-top of Right,
And prove a blessing when naught else can bless. .
Beside how glad the flight, to feel or guess
In such free air the God-likeness of things
Is to desire them: the serene impress
Of beauty's there, the ideal's habitings,
The poet's proper world who lives the song he sings.

## VII

## YOUTH AND AMBITION

O, give! give back my youth! stay, tyrant Time,
Vampire of life! necessity or lust,
Now yield the pregnant treasures of my prime,
Take back the burden of this empty dust,
This sterile promise, this corroding rust,
These fading, jaded memories of joy!
Surrender back my unsuspecting trust,
My hope, health, ecstacy, when a free boy,
Wide rolled and high my earth and ever beauteous toy.

Beam Life upon Earth's ocean-bounded plain,
The silent, ashen sepulcher of man,
That bursts and blooms with natal sweets again
As tho' its varied page had just began:
No mortal mind can multiply its span—
Like to a plant that mounts a mouldered pile,
And growing girds and hides the parent plan,
So youth upon the waiting world doth smile,
And Winter hides his face 'neath Spring's o'erflowing Nile

Now does the heart grow glad and life most sweet,
And stung with interest like a roseate dream:
Tho' ragged steeps have stayed my early feet,
And deep gulfs mocked my march with a faint gleam
Of light to beckon on, yet did I deem
Them proper, nor wept the while my hours,
Dragged into years: for it did often seem
That storms were Life's true preludes 'stead of showers,
That paths are oftimes rough that lead to golden bowers.

Arise, then, Comrade! grasp the living Now!
Scale patiently and high and as a knight
Of noble lineage die ere you bow
To faithlessness: preserve your harness bright,
And to the end maintain a shining fight.
But seek not bliss until your race be run;
If run in gloom, more sweet will be the light;
The highest crown is that the bravest won
The best reward—the laureled canticle, "well done!"

## VIII

### "O, WOMAN'S EYES"

O, Woman's eyes are so bewitching bright,
And her swift tones, so eloquently dear,
Her smile, how full of deep and strange delight,
Her presence how aglow with roseate cheer,
Her mem'ry keen as fire afar or near. .
But ah, the checkered life that she does live,
Commingling day with darkness, hope with fear,
Stern verdicts naming oft but to reprieve,
And casting deep and wide her stars that glad and grieve.

POEMS FROM THE PACIFIC

    Forsooth, what witch more quick with winning ways?
    What siren armed with more enthralling wiles?
    Now with a glance inspires exultant praise,
    Now with another saucily reviles. .
    Crushes and creates with frowns and smiles,
    Or burning memories or blissful hopes,
    Glad'ning the heart she fatally beguiles,
    Tells it of light—a day that never opes,
Then makes O trebly dark the night through which it gropes.


    But when she's true! Woman's best self is true,
    And tried and trustful as a sea-beat rock!
    Who knowing once 't would seem one ever knew:
    The same alway, confronting every shock
    Of time and tempest and each ribald mock;
    Winning all honor by her faithfulness,
    And tireless care, rich gems, which to unlock,
    Is to rejoice and ride e'en mid distress,
On wings which mount and grow, and mounting grow not less.


    When she is true—when gentle Love is like
    The unvarying sun that 'neath all skies
    Glows surely on—how may her being strike
    From our wrapped souls, each chord that in them lies,
    Converting to a gracious paradise
    The heart's wide world and to supremest light,
    By her bright joys and beaming witcheries,
    Yielding all gladness with exhaustless might,
To ears a heaven of sound, to eyes diviner sight.


    And to the life a flow of nectrous peace,
    That poison-like searches the cunning deep

Of every vein and cell, and will not cease
Till it has left a deluge sweet as sleep,
And calmed the fountains that were wont to weep:
O, Woman's eyes can luminate the gray
That clouds the morning of life's dungeon keep,
And beam along our joy-enamored way,
The meaning of the Night, the motive of the day.

# SONNETS

## I

### SAPPHO

Alas! that Love's lit torch should burn in vain,
That Fate should cut off eloquent desire,
Call forth despair as chorus to thy strain,
And choke with grief where sweet breaths did respire,
Or feed with death lost passion's icy pyre!
Thy lyre and love and lot do yet remain,
The tenth invoked magician of all time!
And the glad muse shall through all æons climb. .
Love that was thine ignite, inspire, redeem,
Song that was thine make Beauty more sublime. .
Ah, destiny that named thy life a dream
Has mocked himself and given the world a theme!

## II

## BYRON

A mountain torrent with exhaustless source,
Apalling as it hastens to supply,
An Ætnean flame with undefined course,
Resplendent in its wild sublimity;
A power of varied will now low, now high,
Charming and cursing with acutest force,
Far fastening its spell of cunning art,
To gratify, then prey upon the heart;
O, other wonders may unite and blend,
But this was not itself lest wide apart!
Lord of an height none other could transcend,
With its wild loves and will that would not bend.

## III

## LINCOLN

A champion of humanity and right,
A man of virtue and of simple thought,
Daring for justice with a deep delight,
Nor trumpeting what happily he wrought;
And day by day an honest duty sought;
Wielding high charges with unwearied might,
And by good will won laurels as he rose,
The stronger love of friends and friends of foes;
Such are the foremost of the hero brood,
To such a nation her affection owes:
Whose works are seeds that ever are renewed,
Whose lives are battles for the common good.

## IV

## WOMAN

Chased with fine gold her woman's page appears,
And her rich path with an abundant bliss;
Deny her not the gentleness she rears,
Praise when aright, forgiveness when amiss,
Else cast her o'er despair's unknown abyss,
Or add fresh fuel to her aching fears:
Blest partner! nay, she is life's very source;
Dispensing not alone the nectrous course
To the frail bud she bears, but to the swain,
The hero and the sage, with happy force,
Grants a perpetual summer to sustain,
Life's sweetest stream from an exhaustless vein.

## V

## FREEDOM

The star-democracy that sprinkles space,
The airy reaches of untutored seas,
The leaping seasons' unconstrained race—
Thou art the breath and sinewy soul of these,
The burden of their myriad harmonies,
Rehearsed in whisper soft or thunder bass
O, in the rounds of thy untiring flight
Cleave the cold walk of iron-footed night,
And deeply search the leaden hearts of men,
That they from stars, seas, seasons learn their Right,
Lest drooping, faltering hope expire, and then
Exultant chains may mock the might have been.

## VI

### TO ANNE

When Venus 'rose, the issue of a flower,
Above the silvery mists that veiled the sea,
She wore no charms of a diviner power
Than thine, sweet Anne, are allowed by me;
And my soul sighs an humble prayer to thee—
Most fair enchantress of this midnight hour—
That with thy smiles thou'lt make my darkness light,
Create a day to reign where now is night;
Dispel the forlorn humor of my frame
With the abundance of thy beauty's might . .
Grant thy sweet seal that I may free my flame,
And lock within my heart thy heart and name.

## VII

### TO FESTUS

The deep, warm summers of a liquid love—
The leaping beauty of a young, glad soul—
The web of life that Love and Beauty wove—
I pour to thee and thine and drain the bowl!
Who hast sung the Song and touched the laurel goal,
Who hast won the Bliss when gods have vainly strove,
Oh, drink who can th' insane lees of life!
With ecstacy the laurel of the strife. .
Let reason be thy great Love's prisoner,
And know the sweetness Christ has made thy wife,
The Beautiful that is thy minister—
Thou hast a sure redeemer—it is her!

## VIII

### NIGHT

Inspired Teacher of the gift of Day,
And life's sweet peace, how doth thy coming bless,
And reassure the glory of thy sway;
Grand is thy presence, but thy strong address
Majestic, woos by its stern tenderness,
And mitigates my else distracted way;
Here let the pilgrim bare his burning brow,
And hide in thy dear robe the day's last throe,
For thou canst charge with health and hope and teach
With voice divine, forgetfulness of woe;
Or when mild moons thy wilder forms impeach,
Assert anew how far thy balm may reach.

# SONGS AND BALLADS

# SONGS AND BALLADS

## "HOW BRIGHTLY ON THE LAUGHING RIVER"

Ah me, how brightly on the laughing river
   The liquid summer of thine eyelids shine;
How fair is earth since thou, love, art the giver
      Of light divine!

Each ev'ry airy step of life rejoices
   And every month is quick and young as June,
Since thou, sweet, woke the whole year's yearning voices
      And taught them tune.

Joy swells the air, from cricket to the starling,
   O, sweet, swift music of the tongue of time!
All things have caught the laughter of my darling—
      And learned to rhyme.

And ev'ry flower has blushed in brighter glory
   'Neath the red lips of this supremest queen;
And beaming skies glad trace the painted story
      Of fair Faustine.

The jocund path of day from morn to even
   Is strewn with roseate raptures all the way:
The sparkling joys and jewels of her heaven—
      Like stars at play.

Sweet life! O, glide thou ever to this measure;
   Move thou as this same singing sunlight moves,
The perfect touch of earth's supremest treasure—
      My love of loves!

## FOR AN ALBUM

A name penned on a fading page,
   A name drawn on the drifting shore,
May live a little empty age,
   Then be the blank it was before;
But who engraves upon the mind
   Some darling deed or bless-ed thought,
Shall grasp the happy arts that bind,
   And win the deathlessness he sought.

## "IF A MAN STAND UP TO THE STORM LIKE A MAN"

*Song of the Boatswain.*

If a man stands up to th' storm like a man,
   He will think not much of the end;
He will do his duty as best he can,
   Let it win him foe or friend.

'Twere enough to know what were best to do,
   The right true thing to be done;
The good of many the good of few,
   And the good of every one.

Then when the hands have bestowed their boon,
   And the heart has outpoured its prayer,
What matters it, lads, how late or how soon
   We become as a breath of air?

In your own souls' deep is the sweet of worth,
   And you need no other prize;
Let your conscience be your reward on earth,
   'Twill glad you again in the skies.

No alarms at the last, no chiding train
   Will vex the breast with affright;
It will have no room for the storm of pain
   When filled with the calm of right.

And Death may appear and perfect his plan,
   You are ready whene'er he shall send;
If a man stand up to the storm like a man,
   He will think not much of the end.

## "SWIFT MAY THE TUNE OF SPRING"

Swift may the tune of Spring,
Joy without measure sing
   Fair love for thee:
For thee the blithesome birds,
Weave a sweet trance of words—
   For thee.

Bright trips the silver shoon
Of morn to golden noon,
    Smiling for thee,
Cupids of rosy eve
Fierce dreams of color weave—
    For thee.

White rose and daisies bright,
Lure thee with stars of light,
    Whiter for thee;
Charmed breath of flowers fair
Sweetens the earth and air—
    For thee.

All the young hills rejoice,
Bounding with lusty voice,
    Joyous for thee;
For thee the purple round
Of sight, of sense, of sound—
    For thee.

---

## PSALM OF COURAGE

Alas, for the burden of sorrow,
  For the canker that mixes with clay:
Alas, for the toils of to-morrow
  That are born of the toils of to-day;
Ah, the fact of life's bitter waters,
  The iron-frozen fact of her bain,
The fact that her sons and her daughters
  Are born in a manger of pain.

What then, oh ye that are human,
   Endowed with the lordship of Earth,
What are they now, false men or truemen,
   That heed not the rank of their birth?
The brute in the cold forest meshes
   Wears a nature defiantly warm,
And dares his severest distresses
   In the lap of the sun and the storm.


Oh, say, are ye greater than these are?
   I charge ye arise and come forth;
The head should be high as the lees are,
   And Man be the standard of Worth;
I charge ye come forth where the storm is,
   Assert of what stuff ye are made,
For the God of all gods in your form is,
   In your eye is the lightning of shade.


Ah, treason and trial and trouble,
   Afflictions that come while they go!
If life is a sea that is double,
   Its larger half weighted with woe—
Why, what is the work that availeth,
   What old thing may master the new?
'Tis the ready, stout will that assaileth—
   The Force that finds Duty to do.


Nor grief with its channels of bitter,
   Nor passion that dies in the night,
May wear down the walls that are fitter
   As courts of the cunning of Might;

All life dulls the scythes that are slaying,
    All nature opposes her end,
Let man challenge human decaying,
    And Friendship find out her own friend.

Nay, not as brutality's Nero
    Redress you the ills that are rife,
But be you your own gentle hero
    Resisting the torments of life,
Firm-footed as cedars of red are,
    Great-hearted as mountains of stone;
If fighting where only the dead are,
    O, bear on the battle alone!

All hail to the eloquent story!
    And bind up the wounds that are riven,
Let Manhood assert its brave glory,
    And Womanhood triumph its heaven;
Now staunch ye the tears that like lead are,
    And turn them to gold of the bone;
If fighting where only the dead are
    Oh, bear on the battle alone!

## "O WHENCE THE DELIGHT OF THY FACE"

O, whence the delight of thy face, my love,
    And lustre that haunts thine eye?
Mayhap the fairies of morning wove
This rose of dawn and white of the dove
In fire so fierce as to mock and move
    The soul of the jealous sky!

O, whence thy summer of sound, my own,
   And muse that sings in thy mouth?
Mayhap the birds of spring have flown
To thy lips with roseate wreaths of tone,
Till the breath of thy siren speech has grown
   A symphony of the South.

O whence thy passion of joy, Ma Belle,
   And wealth of gladness to me?
Mayhap the tunes of the morn can tell
Why the sky has wrought its charms in thy spell,
And the air its sweets with the song and swell
   And mystery of the sea!

---

## MIGNON

Bright are the crystal stars and gay,
O, bright the diamond's vital ray,
The lakelet bright 'neath a silvery moon;
Brighter than these or the sheen of noon
   Are the eyes of dear Mignon.

Sweet is the virgin breath of Spring,
Sweet the burdens the bee doth bring,
Sweet is the kiss of the honeyed flower,
Sweeter than either in living power
   Are the lips of my Mignon.

Soft are the snowy folds of the rose,
The mossy bed whereon dews repose,
Soft the white plumage of the swan;
Softer and whiter than silken down
   Is the breast of pure Mignon.

Fine are the hymns in the leafy vale,
Rich the red tones of the nightingale,
Dear is the song of the rippling rill;
But finer and richer and dearer still
    Is the voice of sweet Mignon.

Pure is the blossom and bud new born,
Pure the luculent beads of morn,
The lily pure and feathery foam;
But purer far in its happy home
    Is the heart of loved Mignon.

## "THY WRONGS HAVE MADE THEE SACRED"

Thy wrongs have made thee sacred, lady mine,
And the swift poisons that about thee twine,
    Chilling thy gentle heart,
Climb also to my heart with bitter tread,
As they would sting it too till it were dead,
    Slaying with cruel smart.

No flower, late radiant with enamored light,
Stricken and lone in loneliness of night,
    Nor wounded, mateless bird,
Whose wing could soar no further than its song,
Is half so woful in its weeds of wrong
    As thou whose sigh I heard.

How would I shield thee from the rude world's touch,
The sharp, cold thorns that tear thy life so much,
    How comfort thee with balm

Of gentle words and ministries of love,
  As I would woo an injured, trembling dove,
     Forth from the storm to calm;

And heal thy broken heart with myrrh of rest,
And with new faiths emparadise thy breast,
     So wofully deceived,
Till thou should'st rise glad-winged from life's alloy,
And in the summer of thy white soul's joy
     Forget that thou hast grieved.

## LOVE'S OMNIPRESENCE

When Day forgets his beams,
  And laughing stars illuminate the sea;
When Silence weaves the landscape into dreams,
  And Odor sweet exhales her witchery;
Forth from all these a force more potent springs,
The Love, the sense, the strength, the soul of things.

At Midnight's deeper hour,
  When Earth is 'mid the story of her sleep,
Love's lids hide not her omnipresent power;
  Love is awake, to worship and to weep,
To woo, to warm, sanctify, to calm,
To heal all wounds with heaven-impregnate balm.

As blushes forth the morn,
  With rosy youth aleap from height to height,
The sovereign Sun arises newly born,
  And bathes the world with Love-enchanted light,
Thrilling all life with her supreme caress.
Love is all-where to quicken and to bless.

## "SWEET MEMORIES OF OTHER DAYS"

Sweet memories of other days
   Are sprinkled o'er this hallowed spot,
I walk again the olden ways,
   And live anew the olden lot.

The cradle whence I woke from night,
   When Life's first toysome scenes unfurled,
The wondrous window by whose light
   I first looked out upon the world;

The lads who joined in shout and song,
   The little maids, each ta'en to wife,
That here drew lots for right or wrong,
   And entered on the play of Life;

The fields wide-spread with yellow grain,
   The woods with many a tangled bower,
Where first awoke the sense of gain,
   And conquest of the pride of power—

Enchant my awe-awakened breast,
   Aweary with dominion drear,
Whose best pursuit is that sweet rest
   I left upon the threshold here.

Forms of my youth's fair summer-time,
   Swift days whose foot-fall was not felt,
Glad hours of romance and of rhyme,
   As at dear mother's feet we knelt—

Renew me with your magic zest,
   Aweary of this later cheer,
Whose best pursuit is that sweet rest
   I left upon the threshold here.

## "O, WITH A LIGHT HEART AND A MERRY"

AIR: *Where there's a Will there's a Way*

O, with a light heart and a merry,
    We'll laugh at the wrinkles of care,
Since we find that the sour of the cherry
    Is less than the sweet of the pear;
O, what if the day has been dreary,
    And the dark of the night may be long,
We know where's a light that is cheery,
    And how to drown sorrow in song.

O, what if the clouds' silver lining
    Is dimmed with the hope we held most,
The strength that is spent in repining
    Might regain the prize that is lost;
O, Fortune that's surly and sorry,
    May stab with a pain that is sore,
But to soften our nerves with its worry,
    Will cause it to hurt us the more.

O, then be you off, puling Sorrow,
    And drink of white blood where you may,
For a gallant success on to-morrow
    Will be born of the failure to-day;
O, with a light heart and a merry,
    We'll laugh at the wrinkles of care,
Since we find that the sour of the cherry
    Is less than the sweet of the pear.

## MA BELLE!

Since o'er my startled vision it befell,
  A slight pale foot should pass into my heart,
  My waiting life found out from whence to start,
Mayhap found out whence it may end, as well—
    Ma Belle! Ma Belle!

Nay, the quick circle of her eye ends not!
  Nor its most wondrous sorcery of love,
  Nor any sweet that is a child thereof:
Joys me—that my soul's soul is thus begot—
    Oh rapturous lot!

And from the honeyed meshes of the spell,
  I shall go forth as one made strong as ten,
  As one begirt to work some good to men,
And touch with fire the story he shall tell—
    Ma Belle! Ma Belle!

For she's a marvel worker to mankind,
  Kindling the cunning of weak arms, and stout,
  Shedding the essence of fierce life about—
As wee white teeth sowed by the unseen wind—
    Rose gods behind!

A Gabriel of hope named Florimel,
  Typing the force and comfort of sweet things,
  God sent with sweet light on her wings,
And faithful as God's only Abdiel—
    Ma Belle! Ma Belle!

Because she is in her glad wonderhood—
  And wiles by her love's look such blessedness,
  Who stands not ready to obey and bless,
And taste the bliss till now not understood—
    Born of less good.

Her red lips' wish is dear as heaven's shell,
    That tunes the soul to champion fair ways:
One's subtle sweet has leavened endless days,
And one cut off and killed the sting of hell—
    Ma Belle! Ma Belle!

---

## "NOT ALL THE STRINGS THAT THRILL WITH FIRE"

Not all the strings that thrill with fire,
    Well taught in sounds that can rejoice,
Can wake the thralldom of the lyre
    Whose tune is thy divinest voice.

Tho' Earth be fair from sky to sea,
    My eyes knew not the joy of light,
'Till they looked forth and finding thee
    They found the magic gift of sight.

Blest by the summer of thy glance,
    More potent than the lightning's dart.
My soul joins in Life's jocund dance,
    And Hope rejuvenates my heart.

Now do I feel the worth of life,
    Awakened by thy rosy fire,
The motive and reward of strife,
    The glory of sublime desire.

Most sweet to hear most fair to see,
    Most quick with toils of all glad girls,
Yea, I would lose a world for thee,
    Whose love were greater than all worlds.

## MY LOVE'S THE LIFE.

She is brightness to my day-time,
   A star-sun to my night,
My constant, precious ray-time,
   The all I know of light;
My love's the life of color, too,
   Fair Nature's painted tide,
My love's the life of every hue,
   My love is more beside.

O Music, fill thou all my soul —
   My love is in each strain —
Thy rich, red languishings shall roll
   Throughout my breast and brain,
And raise me with a glad rebound —
   O warm, O liquid bride —
My love's the life of burning sound,
   My love is more beside.

Ah, sweetness of the flower-cups,
   And drippings of the vine,
The burden that the bee sups
   Is of this sweet of mine,
Ah, rapture where the lip clings,
   Ripe fruitage deified,
My love's the life of honeyed things,
   My love is more beside.

The odor of the wildwood,
   And perfume of the grove,
Were caught up with her childhood,
   And nurtured with my love,
Ah, brightness, beauty, sweet distress,
   Delights 'till now denied,
My Love's the life of blissfulness,
   My love is more beside.

## THINE EYES

I see strange dreams burn in thine eyes, my dear,
   And mount on roseate ladders far above,
Where silvery palaces of saints appear,
   Where dwells therein the olive and the dove.

Slim shining temples white as sails at sea,
   And scented phantom courts where lovers woo,
Bright realms and forms of fairy fantasie,
   Calmly afloat in airs of pink and blue.

And all about flowers sing sweet lullabys,
   With red lips sing and whisper tender runes
Of rest and happiness, or with blue eyes
   Conjure the birds to mingle with the tunes.

And for soft interlude the white-lipped leaves
   Of tall fair trees, more queenly than the moon,
Chorus apace: and through all Cupid weaves
   His mellow shafts from night to golden noon,

Or swells the love-tuned harmony afar
   Among the exultant hills, or with light wing,
Vibrates with bounding joy from star to star,
   As 'twere the life and soul of things to sing.

Sweet song and breathing scarlet of the Morn!
   And skies with painted gamuts of swift sound!
O, smiles and flowers of tune that heaven adorn!
   Passion and joy of an immortal round!

Joy, Hope, Enchantment pulsate in the spell!
   The lighted cunning of a vast surprise:
And these quick things and more than words can tell,
   Glow in the wondrous thralldom of thine eyes!

## "YOU HAVE SAID THE CHARMED WORDS"

You have said the charmed words that you love me, Ma Belle,
And a roseate light jewels forth with its joy,
    And with bright-bosomed swell
Sweeps the sky as if sped by that fire-arm-ed boy,
And weds the gold Sun where his swift glances toy,
    Rejoicing the day with his spell!


And the air with electrical bound
    Is quick with its story of life!
As if Sol had translated his gold into sound,
And silver-tongued stars joined the eloquent round
    And swelled the melodious strife!
    And waking the morn and the noon,
The hills and the vales with sweet minstrelsy rife
With flowers deck the Bride that young joy takes to wife,
    And dance to the rapturous tune!


    Oh, Bride of the Shore and the Sea,
      The world is re-modeled for me!
Its color and sweetness and sound have new sense,
Its motive and end a divine eloquence,
    That caught its divineness from thee!
The hand hath a cunning undreamed of before,
The heart the joined force of the Sea and the Shore,
    The senses the Strength to be free,
The ear hath sweet gladness to hear evermore,
    And the eye deeper beauty to see!


You have said the charmed words that you love me, Ma Belle,
    And I rise from the desolate dust of the night,
    To where the fierce rose of this life giving light
Cleaves the hateful eclipse of the darkness of hell,
    And paints the proud sky with its message of might—
      "All is well! All is well!"

## "O, HOPE, LIFT UP THY WEARY WINGS"

O, Hope, lift up thy weary wings,
   And make them into lighter ones,
The veriest birdling forward flings
Sweet challenge in the song he sings,
With quick white joys the welkin rings,
   E'en Phœbus hath no whiter ones. .
O, Hope, take up thy barren wings,
   And wake them into brighter ones.

Tiptoe upon the mountain side,
   The Day hath found a fleeter way;
More sparkling flows the brittle tide,
The skies are ope'd more wide and wide,
All things proclaim the waiting Bride,
   All Life doth gladly greet her way,
Tiptoe upon the mountain side,
   The May hath found a sweeter way.

O, Hope, take up thy distant wings
   And make them into nearer ones:
All through the night my dreaming brings
Fierce prophecies of coming things,
When, lo, the morrow's prospect clings
   To wonderscapes of clearer ones. .
O, Hope, take up thy dreary wings,
   And wake them into dearer ones.

I yearn to catch the fuller tone,
   The truest of Love's history:
I burn to clasp the magic zone
Of Summer ere her sweets have flown. .

And I shall have thee, Hope, my own,
   And bear my aching kiss to thee—
I yearn to catch the fuller tone,
   The newest of Love's mystery.

O, Hope, take up thy leaden wings
   And make them into airy ones. .
Thou wilt not cheat me—queen of kings—
With unsubstantial gladennings,
Nay, all my soul en-hungered springs
   To sunny joys and starry ones. .
O, Hope, take up thy earthy wings
   And wake them into fairy ones.

---

## "FAIN WOULD I TELL"

Fain would I tell my idol some sweet thing,
   But know not how if words must bear the tale;
My love knows not a language it can sing,
   Nor how to arm song-arrows to prevail.

There is a message, deeper, truer, far,
   The still and hallowed Sinai of the soul,
That speaks without an error or a jar,
   Inscribed on an imperishable scroll!

Read that and know, else never may be known,
   Observe with what my ev'ry glance is rife,
Look 'neath an eye that sees but thee alone,
   And view the charm that operates my life.

## "CALL NOT THE PROMISE VAIN"

#### SONG OF THE PIONEER

Call not the promise vain, Camille,
    Call not the prospect dark;
Have we not wealth in rosy health,
    And youth for a sturdy bark?
Is the world not wide with ready work
    For ready hands to do,
And will not my heart play an earnest part
    When invoked by love and you?


Call not the promise vain, Camille,
    Call not the prospect dark;
Is there not life in very strife
    When happiness—the mark?
Is there not strength in the depth and height
    Of bliss we hold in view,
And will not my heart play a noble part
    When inspired by love and you?


Call not the promise vain, Camille,
    Call not the prospect dark,
Let courage bold our lives enfold,
    And labor be our ark;
Is there not cheer in our path of hope,
    Will not success pursue,
And will not my heart play a manly part
    When inflamed by love and you?

## "LET US BE CONSCIOUS HOW HAPPY WE ARE"

Let us be conscious how happy we are,
   That the summer of life is our own,
The winter that chills and the shadows that mar
   Have warmed in the stars that have shone;
Our years are as acts of a joyous dream,
   Our moments as rays of a sun,
Our lives are the flood of a master stream—
   Two streams that have mingled in one.

Let us be conscious how happy we are,
   For contentment has sweetened our earth;
To the crowd we resign the discords that jar,
   To the desert surrender its dearth;
We have learned to fathom the deeps of our day,
   Have caught the fine music of things,
We have courted the burden of sweets on our way,
   And conquered its burden of stings.

## "LOOK UP POOR HEART"

Look up, poor heart, the night is nearly past,
   Plod yet a little thy impatient way,
A shining joy awaits thee at the last,
   Earth was thy Night, but heaven will be thy Day.

Look up, dear heart, the dawn is nearly come,
   Be greater than thy burthen yet a space,
Each mocking step conveys thee nearer home,
   Each drop of sweat begems thy final place.

> Look up, good heart, sweet Death is near at hand!
>     Be firm and true until he bid thee rise,
> And for thy valor grant with magic wand
>     The burthen of the blisses of the skies!

---

## "FINE WAS HIS VOICE WHOSE RUDDY LIP"

> Fine was his voice whose ruddy lip
>     The Hebla bees once sought to sip,
>         And sweet the tone
>     The siren wings from her fatal throne..
> But finer far the finished tongue,
> And sweeter far the silver lung
>     That spells my darling's name..
> That holds fierce mem'ries in serene control,
> And echoes gladness to my deepest soul—
>         "*Minne!*"
>     The beauty-flame,
>     That spells this pregnant name.

>         Fast to the voice's wing
>         A thousand graces cling
>         Caught from mine own..
> Spells of dear light that round her eyelids shone,
> Sweet couriers of the thralldom of her throne,
> Singing sweet calm into the inmost heart,
>         An halcyon delight,
> A joy her flowering beauty doth impart
>         With soft entrancing might,
> And while forgetful of all else beside,
> It renders smooth the breast of pleasure's tide.

And thus it sings—
That inner tongue—and here the tale it brings. .

"Fair! Fair!
To Beauty's despair,
As she were born in the womb of the rose,
And nursed by the snows. .
The light of the skies is dyed in her hair—
Fair! Fair!"

"Sweet! Sweet!
From face unto feet,
Her tinted charms are mistaken for flowers;
Like myrrh are her hours,
Her blisses more keen than nectar of wheat—
Sweet! Sweet!"

And it fills with rapture the moment's space,
With a theme as bright as a comet's face—
None fitter to rejoice—
And the beautiful line of her life I trace
By advices from the voice,
Which holds quick mem'ries in serene control,
And echoes gladness to my deepest soul—
"*Minne!*"
The beauty-flame,
That spells this pregnant name.

## "IF DREAMS HAVE TONGUES"

### TO YOLONDE

If dreams have tongues, then a dream may tell,
A joy that has painted my heart, Ma Belle,
When the sun went out with his red wings furled,
But left thy light to illume the world :
And hope has templed my roseate sky
'Neath the gamut of color that haunts thine eye,
And the clouds of Night are how vainly curled
When thy light is left to illume the world.

Ah, the dreams that are full of the sweet of this!
The red of bloom and the scarlet of bliss!
The Cupids that lie in thy fierce caress!
The prodigal fire of thy golden tress!
Yea, they found the sting of life and its sweet
Was in wooing here at thy lily feet,
That the flames of the world's applause were less
Than the prodigal fire of thy golden tress!

## "CEASE THY TREMULOUS PLAINT"

Nay, cease thy tremulous plaint,
My tender-bosomed mate, my sweet, my saint,
And nestle close while I confirm thy trust,
And frighten from thee each delusive fear,
And stay the dawning sparkle of each tear,
Pleading a love whose deathless name is *must*.

Thou whom I took to me,
The first wife-portion of my destiny,
Responsive to each love-prayer of my heart,
Think not the bond so brittle as to break,
That thou wilt from thy precious rest awake;
Thy soul and mine have not learned how to part.

Nay, on life's fickle tide
Thou, sweet, shalt be my ever-present bride,
The object of a changeless tenderness,
Whose flower-like frame can be as easy chilled,
Whose gentle breast with pain as fully filled,
As when I took thy hand and swore to bless.

If we be not one voice,
Or there be error somewhere in our choice
Which it were wretchedness to alter now—
We will maintain the honor of our deeds,
And prove heroic to their sternest needs,
For Love doth oft re-crown a noble brow.

Howbeit rest in peace,
And dare all thought but of our lives' release;
Together we our wedded steps shall wend,
Be each the other's counterpoise of strength,
Together test this life's elastic length,
Together try the riddle of its end!

# MISCELLANEOUS

# MISCELLANEOUS

## SIERRA'S GOOD-NIGHT TO THE SUN-GOD *

A golden flame Sierra's crest illumes,
In massive conflagration, triple bright,
As o'er its trembling jewels of sleek ice,
The Day-King bursts—a cataract of fire!

And thus to the World's Lamp, ere his last kiss
Of mellow light had died—Sierra spoke.

"O, thou, whose smile is Day, whose absence Night,
Pythagoras hath sung thy pregnant names,
And ev'ry time and tongue hath hailed thee God!
I, too, am crowned, since of the Occident,
Thou, the World's Eye, beam'st last upon my brow!

"Supremest Author! Parent! Father! Lord!
Alpha of being, Omega of bliss!
I, parting, do salute thee worshiping!
With thy quick key of gold hast thou unlocked
The hidden wombs of earth, and lo! in pride,
Blossomed the painted miracles of Time!

---

*The Sierra Nevada Range, though situated over a hundred miles inland, is so much higher than the Coast Range its peaks receive the last rays of the sun upon the estern continent.

In red and bronze and purple, luscious fruits,
And grain in waves of yellow light ablaze,
And, tenderest of all, thy burning touch,
In poesy of flowers did pulsate,
And crimsoned of thy veins, did beam and blush
The rose—to make men glad!


" Resplendent Sol!
Most ancient Giver of sweet shining Life!
With Titan glory traversing thy twelve
Celestial signs, thy Labors, copied by
Chaldean Ur and Grecian Hercules,
Sublimely move the world with tread of song!
Thou art Time's mighty Tune! From thee, Bright God!
Thy singing son the Lyre inherited,
That Music's touch might build earth's walls, and chord
The race of Man with universal Good!


" From thee, the state of Harmony! the place
Where man and nature blend in rhythmic peace,
The spectrum of the cosmic consciousness!
The victory of Love is thine—espoused
Of heaven—and mightier than Death or Time!
Love! the supremest beaming Godliness?
Wooing to rest all things storm-rent and sad,
Sheathing the spent sword of unripe evil,
And with breath of healthful honeyed magic,
Creating men in the grand mould of Gods!
O, sweet translation! transfiguration august!
Most wondrous fair glad mystery of Life!
How sparkles forth the lighted flame of sense,
With bliss 'til now undreamed, and passionate
'Neath the strange gaze of beaming paradise!

"Pearl chastening Sun! the diamond hath stored
Thine eye-light in its heart; the opal's torch,
The sapphire's blue, the ruby's mirrored blood,
Hath caught the shining laughter of thy face,
And live, transcendent Horus, in thy love;
Earth's emerald sward, the fields of daffodil,
The purple heath are of thy countenance;
And all the landscapes happiness, and the seas,
The electric flash of silvery scales,
And on the dreamy undulating downs,
The glint of butterflies, and curving flight
Of vari-plumaged birds, were in thine
Eye-flash born to honor thee!

"O, Fire-King!
Vulcan or Mars, Elias or Apollo,
From the Aurorean blushes of the dawn,
To burning Hesperus, thou fill'st the world
With Glory and with God! O, Circle Lord!
O, deathless central Unity of Things!
Life's Yesterday! To-day! To-morrow! thou!
Or if, at last, the lagging sands of Earth
Shall cease to tempt the catholic tread of Man,
Weary of weaving threads of scarlet Life,
In thy embrace shall again be garnered,
Each atom's form to be re-born of thee!


Farewell, O Brilliant Phœbus! thy maiden Night
Doth beckon as thy purple smile doth wane,
And from this fittest shrine, this mountain altar,
I, with religious homage cry aloud,
Good-night to thee! A continent's Good-night!"

## CLARA FOLTZ

### JURIST—MOTHER—WOMAN

The Forum's breath is hushed and still;
    Pacific's Portia awes the scene!
And conscious echoes throb and thrill,
The list'ning spaces fright and fill
    With thunders from the Apennine!
Invective, logic, wit, are here,
    The patriot spirit of our laws,
And by her periods keen and clear
The good are freed, the guilty fear
    The towering triumph of her cause.

But what new tone has that voice found,
    Upon which silent thousands hung?
About fair blossoming babes are wound
Lispings of love—a trance of sound,
    The Gracchi mother's hymn re-sung;
A jurist—mother—teacher now,
    The eagle mellowed to the dove;
Upon each rare and radiant brow
The honest worth of pen or plow
    Is blazoned by the kiss of love!

Amidst it all this empress born,
    Pursued her lofty woman's way;
Evil was shamed beneath her scorn,
And jeweled like the shining morn
    Were the acts of all her day;
A kiss gave she for every blow,
    A smile she had where shadows vex;
She was where'er her feet did go
The chasteness of the whited snow,
    The swan-like Leda of her sex.

## HYMN TO THE CALM NIGHT *

The tired spent Day has ceased his busy round
   And seeks the purple silence of repose:
Sweet as love is this hallowed sleep of sound,
   This rest beneath the poppy and the rose.

Most gracious to give o'er the weight of care,
   And close the weary eye-lids from sick sight;
Renew thee, Day, in holy calm of prayer,
   Secure within the fostering arms of Night.

For she's the parent of rebuilded power,
   Strong in her healing as the kiss of Love,
Yet gentle as the breath of maiden-flower,
   And watchful as the patient Mother-Dove.

Let me steal deep into thy bosom's rest,
   And hide the soul too worn to laugh or weep;
Or find in the charmed wonder of thy breast
   The sweet oblivious miracle of sleep.

Yea, fold with wing made soft in Lethe's tide
   All weary things that swoon and swim as dead,
The Wind's low quivering lip hold thou and hide,
   And Echo tell no troubled word he said.

---

the following from the Boston Home Journal:
poem (Hymn to the Calm Night), by Venier Voldo, was written
succeeding a terrific storm in the Sierra Nevada mountains, which
author his life, and was therefore inspired by a spirit of thanksgiving.
ss of its poetic feeling and beauty of diction bear lofty testimony for
poet."                     [THE PUBLISHERS.]

Oh, mighty Night! still thy dark might as Death!
  Half mover of the world—yet wondrous still;
All fair time's fruitage sweetens on thy breath,
  Bright woven in the summer of thy will.

Most darling armistice 'mid life's fierce fray,
  Missioned with myrrh and secret-scented charms,
Each brow hard flushed with victory of the day,
  Glad seeks the soft refreshment of thine arms.

Smoothed all the tortured vesture of the face,
  And the faint heart has stilled his fev'rish throe,
The red life-stream has paled his passion-trace,
  And stayed the headlong fervor of his flow.

The village dreams, and hushed the city's hum,
  The shadows mass and sleepy star-lights gleam;
The strength of Speech finds out its strength while dumb,
  And Progress draws her castles from a dream.

The breath of all the world, how soft and low,
  As Night hath come to weep o'er some loved bier;
The lazy pine-plumes swaying to and fro
  Refuse their vespers to the listening ear.

Yea, sound is shamed away and will not speak,
  Save the dull drops whose mournful monody
Pours ever from yon cavern's mantled cheek,
  To swell the sobbing pæans of the sea.

And all forgetful of his faltering staff,
  The bald grandsire hath donned a wing-ed shoon;
Where late were flying feet and rippling laugh,
  The step of morning and the voice of noon.

Deep in the solemn vistas of the vale,
   Or far within the cloisters of the wood,
Tired beast and bird have quit th' exhausted trail
   To still the lair or shield the sleeping brood.

O'er the pale hills the half moon's mellow beams,
   Lay like a ghostly glamour o'er things dead;
And gild yon pensive, meditative streams,
   With light as tender as of eyes just wed.

Lo, all hath yielded to the trance of Peace!
   Not death is here, but life in sternest power,
With silent, earnest tread that will not cease,
   As time hung from the cradle of an hour.

Oh, youth-renewing Night, praised be thy calm!
   All praised the reposeful measure of thy sway!
The rent soul heal with thy benignest balm,
   And touch December with the wand of May.

Teach us, O Night, to know thee as thou art,
   The one supremest dignity of earth;
And in thy presence elevate the heart,
   To feel the sense of a sublimer worth.

Now Peace be still. . sweet harbinger of life!
   Now Peace be still. . the olive is abroad!
And Sleep shall find this sabbath-time of strife
   The Benediction of a sleepless God!

This be the sacrament of silent love,
   And token of the everlasting calm!

Oh, he who understands—him shall it prove,
   And win the worship of a voiceless psalm;

Or with thanksgiving flood the shining soul;.
   Sweet Night, my love is less than should have been,
Be thou more near and from my life unroll
   The glad religion of good will to men.

## GOOD-SPEED TO MEN

Speed ye, Good-speed, upon the race of life,
   To all men speed and gracious stars and song!
The strife of good—let that become the strife,
   And all forget one thing—forget to wrong.

Alas! there is enough that needs must be
   To mock at hope and cross our anxious way;
Let no hand then afflict the prostrate knee,
   No wanton shadow fill the room of day.

'T were better to raise up this troubled thing,
   And brush some burden from her onward path;
To cheer a soul is easy as to wring,
   And tender courage stronger is than wrath.

Bid him Good-speed, the struggling child of pain,
   By wrong or error or misfortune won;
He needs no more cold links upon his chain,
   Nor added gauntlets of despair to run.

He is most man who blesses as he goes,
   Most woman who inspires divinest deeds;
Who circumscribes the awful waste of woes,
   Who heals—as woman can—the soul that bleeds.

Peace, peace on earth, Good-will, Good-speed to men!
   All hail and triumph now and to the end,
The endless end, when hope is won, and when
   Great man finds man the universal friend!

## YOLONDE WITH THE YELLOW HAIR

Fairest of all fierce gifts of life I found
   Yolonde with the yellow hair . .
. Her, the conflagration of the soul,
The glad foam-dream made burning flesh again,
     Star-browed and fair,
Forth broke from the embraces of the night.

And it were hard for more of joy to be!
What of the scented airs of Idumæa
   Or charm-songs that the siren choir
   Have sweetened of the singing spheres?
To me she is the burden of all sweets,
With exhalations of the youthful morn,
   And music soft as Lydia's.

Suffer me right near to you Yolonde,
   For distance is despair . . .
To quit you then were one thing more—despair!
Your being hath a wealth of witchery
Fired by that magician of the heart
   That turneth peace to madness . . .
There are strange odorous stings about you
   Caught mayhap from incense-atmospheres,
   The perfume-worship of Greek goddesses . .
And they steal forth with every move of you;
   From your eyes' lucid eloquence;
   Beneath your pregnant touches;

The draperies that hide your awful riches;
Your hair . . your sharp wan hair, Yolonde!
What young glad suns lent you their gold
      To stain it—the crown
Whose silken scepter sways by Beauty's force,
Cast forth in grace like circling comet-light?


But how in this same yellow hair, Yolonde,
  ·Shall I find rest and calm of life?·
  I may lie in it drunken
And helpless beneath your fascination . .
  Alas! there were such peril then,
    Lest on your breasts—
Falling in a charmed surrender—
My life shall hold its breath, and go!
  Ceasing to be—for ecstasy.


Or in the vibrations of strange chords,
  The inner temple's muse,
Sweet as the love-lisps of angelic tongues,
  Whence, my white captor, have you come,
  Whither dost lead me with your sorcery,
  And wherefore to my proud repletion?
Am I not full enough of you,
Having you at my soul's anchorage,
  And where my spirit fastens to its God?
Well, you are and must be, th' interpreter,
  Of all of this deep mystery;
Illumining my labyrinthine way,
Crossed and up-ploughed by dragon-teeth,
Until I find, by you and with you,
  The august, awful destiny!

I saw you yester eve in Fancy's world,
   The best and loveliest thing I could create ..
To-day I hold you as a heaven won,
And have you to my selfish self—
   Lost in you or saved—
As you were th' eternal consciousness!
     To-morrow—what?
It cannot be without your presence
Preying upon the vitals of my life—
   Further I dare not question:
To-morrow is loving Death's and Life's,
   The unknowable Nirvana!
   The oblivion of Rest!
   The———

# THE MINISTRY OF NATURE

#### A FRAGMENT

### I

When in the race of life or care or pain
   Weigh heavily upon you or the blight
Of disappointed hope; when come again
   Vague forms of dearer days shedding the light
Of ghostly-seeming bliss, list to a strain
   From nature as her happy haunts invite
Sincere communion, and attempt to feel
The peace, the joy, that she will then reveal.

### II

Go forth alone, confiding, and make her
   Your priest; confess, resolve, amend; there **find**
What you should have, a worthy minister,
   And forms for every taste; have but a mind
To do and be advised; do not incur
   A needless censure, but contrive to bind
In one triumphant whole, apart from strife,
The being, aim and end of earthly life.

### III

There find society without a sting,
   There learn a language of the sweetest tone,

There view the beautiful—a perfect thing,
  There feel companionship with Peace alone,
There hear the melody that angels bring,
  There know the glory that alone is known .
In atmospheres of unity and love,
And 'mid the powers that melt and mould and move.

### IV

Seek one of those bright-painted balmy eves
  That have a vital freshness for the heart;
One that a day of storm so often leaves,
  When Sol's emblazoned blushes slowly part
Their deep'ning hues from eyes their absence grieves:
  When shimmering fires like angel beacons start,
Weaving their scarlet hair with ermine shrouds,
And with strange gold embroidering the clouds

### V

There's then a glory in the trackless wood
  That re-creates us; a sense that in
Its first and highest sympathy with good,
  Inspires profoundest awe; far from the din
Of marts in sacred isolation, why should
  There not exist a presence half divine,
That may be wooed and won—and that instills
A fire celestial in the soul it fills.

### VI

The moon arises and her silvery beams,
  Soft, warm and feminine, steal gently
O'er the hills. . a dream of light; the earth seems
  Filled with heaven's atmosphere; the sentry

Stars with eyes of gold look down on streams,
   And vales, and fields of sheen, marking intently
How all sweet life bestows her varied bliss,
Or Beauty pouts her universal kiss.

### VII

O woodland wild! thou hast a pleasure dear
   To me; a something passionately loved
Ever pervades thy throbbing grandeur here
   In these far depths of solemn shade unroved;
There is an inspiration in thy cheer
   That leaves alone the bristling throng unmoved,
A ratifying grace and bounty given,
That draws the soul to virtue and to heaven.

### VIII

Convert us to thee, Nature! thy kind forms
   Teach more impressively than words of men,
The all beneficence and bliss; bright morn's
   Refreshing gifts; its living breeze to fan
The sweet perfumes; the evening's glow that warms
   Us into rapture; the sky's clear, deep span;
Night's mellow majesty and th' green glad sea,
Conspire to fill our souls with love and thee.

## BIRTH-SONG OF APHRODITE.

I am content that I have conquered Earth!
And charmed her with deep mysteries of my birth
As have my sisters—awful mistresses—
The planets of the spacious airy seas,
The universe of passion and of man!
I am content with heaven's bepurpled plan—
The glorious daughter, I, of Sea and Sun,
Born when the singing stars had just begun;
And Time beheld my shreds of yellow hair;
And bowed before the sovereignty of the Fair.

O, empire sweet of dawning consciousness!
O, pregnant luscious life-flow! if to bless
My being to myself was bless-ed! great!
And gracious! O, proud! O, rapturous estate!
I lay encouched on foam-flowers that rose
And fell in dreamy luxury by flows
Of gentle seas; and fanned with swaying showers
Of poppied fragrance were my young sweet hours;
About festoonings were of fleecy spray,
Winking wee jeweled eyes at stars at play,
Sea kissing Sky in happy ministry . .
Ah, now! the revelation of myself to me!
My snowy nakedness and rounded gifts!
Like creamy marble, save where color sifts
Her dainty blushes through tralucent skin,

With tiny purple stains nestling therein . .
Smooth were all these—my gracious lordly limbs,
And breathing breasts—all smooth and pure as hymns,
Winged now by my staff of sea nymphs . . Ah, joy!
Did I but only with my gold hair toy
Thou wert my own—my gold hair soft and warm,
Prodigal of its voluptuous form,
Or with two alabaster feet, each one
Perfection, with pink toes nodding at the Sun!

And the proud Sea—my mother—ceased from travail;
White flowers o'erspread her bosom, vast and pale,
Aromas fanned her shining face and mine;
She slept as one sleeps languid from much wine,
In trance of bliss—that in begetting me
Glory was hers throughout eternity!
And my great Sire's great face—so glad was it—
Brightened with such glistening smiles as lit
The new earth and skies with a youth of gold. .
Then all the forms of being did behold
My vivid, awful loveliness, and great
The joy of things that Beauty was create!
Joy was above and all about was joy;
Adoring-songs and wrestlings to employ
Divinest ways of worship; and I saw
How I awakened all! the law my law!
And things were beautiful because of me—
The perfect round of my divinity—
And mine were mighty metaphors of praise,
As forth I floated to begin my days.

I am content that I was made so fair;
That fierce stars come to nestle in my hair,

The gentle wavelets with most dear caress
Kiss my fond fingers and my flowing tress,
And soft gold birds and silver fishes come
To sprinkle pleasure round my path of foam:
Mayhap yon tissuey cloudlets would not flirt
Bright faced and happy about Iris' skirt—
The wonder painted goddess of the skies—
But to make little raptures for my eyes;
Nor but for me would yonder landscapes fair,
Breathe their swift passions to the wanton air,
Yon green-haired glades and vales with shining face,
Glide into heaven with calm luxuriant grace. .
All things, indeed, are charmful for of me;
Yea! Color stole from me her mystery!
And blushed to the faces of her flower-waifs,
O'er the pink walls of shell palaces and reefs
Of vari-tinted coral; o'er the streams
Of scarlet glory when my Sire sinks to dreams
In his Sea's embrace, or arises thence:
And I it was who woke magniloquence;
Taught the musicians of the Sea their strains,
The shell-songs their tune, gave the waves the reins
Of melody and the winds their plaintive sighs,
The winged things of the air their minstrelsies;
Born was the muse of every sound that sings
Of my vocal womb and woman-whisperings!

I am content that I have conquered Earth!
And made Life date its sweetness from my birth!
Its sweetness and its meaning and its cause,
And Love find out the thralldom of his laws,
Death lose his sting and victory by me—
The glory, glow and gladness of the Sea!

# SEVEN SISTERS

### MARY

The eldest was of splendid dignity,
With form of slender finish and a grace
Caught from the presence of the queenly pine;
Maturely calm and gracious was her air,
Or beaming with restrained religious light,
How gentler than the glory of the moon.
Her words were as the manna of fair speech
That hungry ears delight to hang upon,
Cheered and exalted by a goodly muse;
The eldest and the most reposeful, she,
Observing that men suffer and are blind,
And by sweet acts of good made all men feel
The holy sphere of lady—woman—wife!

### HATTIE

Nature to Hattie was less prodigal,
Save as to mind; which shining, happily,
From patient culture and adornment rare,
Was as a trimmed lamp in benighted ways;
Her speech asparkle with the life of wit
Was like the infectious soul of wine or fire,
At once the hope and courage of brave lives:
Stainless her smile as joyous was her laugh,
Her heart as tender as a violet's breath,
Her modesty as gentle as the dove.

### EMMA

There was a still demeanor in the maid,
A sweet reserve and self-reposeful pride,
Yet with a happy eloquence of act
That seemed like noblest charity at last;
Hers was a quiet tenderness and care
That sued a cloistered silence for its use,
But like Ruth's deeds with deep pure zeal bestowed;
Her peasant blush was fair as chastity,
For from pure Dian's lip the tint was ta'en,
And traced as o'er the features of a rose.

### CLARA

A bland brunette—twin-sister to the last,
And twin to the fair god of gentle Love!
Her great glad eyes conjured the bright gazelle,
But more than these her grace; like Saadi's clay—
Which when encountered bears perfume so long—
Her magic presence wrought an influence deep,
And fraught with blessedness; and her joy-lit path
Graced with a life's white purity and truth,
Was well the favorite theme of favored friend;
Her voice hymned fervent syllables of good,
And strangely sweet it fell upon the heart,
As 't came from lips with which a Sappho sung.

### CORINNE

All radiant was the conduct of her walk;
Barely in womanhood's beginning,
She stepped the threshold with a goodly strength
Well formed acquirements and a high resolve;

MISCELLANEOUS

Glad was the facial rhetoric she wore,
Full of impressive loveliness and mirth,
With a nobility and chaste delight
So like the bride that Zampieri paints.

### FLORA

She was a blonde—all winning as a flower,
With skin of living and translucent white,
As smooth as lake of Uri's glassy breast;
But sixteen sunny summers had she passed,
Yet now the binding beauty of her parts
Appealed to praise; light was her frequent laugh,
And her cerulean eye, large, round and clear,
Just made responsive to a star's quick smile;
Her silken curls that flirted with the breeze,
And bounding elasticity of step,
Each suited well the lustre of her spring.

### CARRIE

The youngest was a ripple of bright joy;
Brown eyes and hair and pearly teeth were hers,
And an expression fraught with sympathy,—
Inspired of girlish innocence and love;
The child was sensitive beyond her years;
Simple her wishes and her care sincere,
Like Jessica—tho', not undutiful,
With an affection more to woo and win.

\* \* \* \* \* \* \* \*

Observe the tender harmony and grace
That bound this winsome rosary of girls,
As in a magic unison they dwelt,
Belike a well-tuned instrument's accord,

Or single note of an Azazie choir:
No gilded passion lured them from their path;
No pale ambition preyed upon their peace;
They sought their duty without fashion's show,
Nor parleyed with the flippant ranks of pride;
So life did pass them happy as a dream,
As pure and clear as yonder star-beam's light,
And it was shared with others and with good;
Short was the upright wording of their creed—
*To do right for the love of right* was all—
Their earliest lesson and their latest deed.

## "AH! FOR THE LOVE THAT HAS NO VOICE"

But ah! for the love that has no voice,
   That breathlessly flows on its deep, deep way,
   That noiselessly murmurs the live long day,
Pouring its burthens forth to its choice
   In liquid and swelling and nectrous runes,
   And the great grand tongue of unspoken tunes;
O, eyes that talk of a soul within,
   O, eyes that shame the quick stars asleep,
You have won your will that is sweeter than sin,
   And caught my will in the tyrannous deep;
O, sweet abysses of eyes and lips,
   The eyes that charm and the lips that cling,
I know a porch whence poison drips,
   Fierce and sweet with the fire of spring;
And, O, the eloquent, wonderful tales—
   The freighted breath that bears to the skies,
   The wild refrain of her vocal sighs,
Death! I am thine when their pleading fails!

## JULIETTE

My love was born of the womb of hate,
   Alas! for the love thus sadly born,
Alas! for the mark of a barren fate,
   And the cloud that darkened my rosy morn;
That hate—half lovely for love's sake—
   The parent hate slew its offspring love,
But not 'till the martyred thing did make
   Its fate a rebuke of the curse that strove:
Love's breath like a stream of the setting sun,
   Sweetened my veins to my finger tips,
And when our amorous day was done,
   Each died on the other's poisoned lips.

## "I SAW THEE AND I LOVED THEE"

I saw thee and I loved thee!
　But 'twere vain to chase the cunning
Of the mystery that moved me . .

. . .

For the thousand springs that gladdened,
The ten thousand stings that maddened,
　Stayed and held my captured being,
O, were subtler than could ever,
　Ever yield to simple seeing:
All my deep soul's deepest knowing
　Felt and blessed the ministrations,
Knew thy souls sublime o'erflowing,
　Keenly felt its inspirations,
Each profound and pure bestowing,
　With affection's best endeavor,
　And the blessing of a lover.

I saw thee and I loved thee!
　But I cannot tell the secret
Of the mightiness that moved me . .

. . .

For Love in thy tresses nestled,
　Touched the rose-hue of thy cheek,
With thy winning laughter wrestled,
　Thy glad habits that could speak,

Love provoked thy tongue's persuasions,
   Lit the torches of thine eyes,
Moved thy touch's minstrations,
   And thy motions' melodies,
And the atmosphere about thee,
Had been loveless if without thee,
   And the magnet so imbedded
   In the presence I had wedded,
Drew me with a power to thee
'Till my deepest soul did woo thee.

I saw thee and I loved thee!
   But 't were vain to seek the meaning
Of the ministry that moved me.

## THE COMEDY OF EVIL

Some lives will not learn but of leaves of pain,
    Of letters of iron and words of frost,
That live to-day because yesterday slain,
    And are saved because they were sorely lost.

The laws of life are many, my child,
    And far more deep than the strange deep sea,
And are most calm seéming most to be wild,
    And most controlled where they seem most free.

Forth from a perilous, pitiful Night
    To the fiercely rapturous arms of Day . .
O, wayward storms of a black hell-light,
O, Sphinx whose eyes wear the nightmare of sight—
    Delusive lie of a wonderful way—

Your work is done with its terrible good,
    Its Power, its Cleanliness, Patience and Truth,
    The gray of your age is the gold of my youth,
And the rod is resolved into sceptre-hood!

O, Comedy strange! O, Lethean Life!
    That measures bliss by the red white blood,
That leads to Peace by the Path of Strife,
    Says to unripe Evil " mature to Good."

Ah, man cannot live by bread alone,
  He shall taste of the whole great various Earth—
  One prodigal thing were akin to dearth—
And a surfeit of light were worse than none.

To lose one's way and to find it anew,
  To hurt one's friend with the heel of might,
Is the plan that maketh the false ways true,
  The shame that teacheth the wrong heart right. .

Some lives will not learn but of leaves of pain,
  Of letters of iron and words of frost,
That live to-day because yesterday slain,
  And are saved because they were sorely lost.

MISCELLANEOUS

## APHRODITIS—A PASSION MONODY

### TO YOLONDE

Who hath become godlike in Love's lore—
 The deeps of love-sighs having sounded,
 Or proved the purple travail in the veins
That story forth the mysteries of bliss?


 O, Woman! type of beautiful divineness!
 Th' incarnate rapturous Cause art thou—
 Astarte, Juno or the Ark of worlds!


And if it be a bitter thing—yet will I love,
 And weep in Love's Gethsemane,
Arising thence on sovereign wings of fire
As one enamored of the light of life . .
I worship God in this strange worship,
 And feel his vivid gloriousness:
His sharp breath touching my life-strings
With sweetest pæans of repose . .
 Becalmed else on Love's fair breast and His,
'Neath gentlest palpitations of white heaven,
I rest in the Nirvana of the soul.


Bright inspirations touch my line of life
  Like jewels on a star-path;
 Una or undying Florina,
Yolonde, Urline, Ælæa or Glaphira—

'Tis a communing with my greater self,
  As stars do with their suns—
My soul-wife, the feminine of my being,
My counterpoise unto a balanced whole..
  Her influence is a scented spell,
That steals unto the subtlest depths of me,
  Till I am lost in sweet duality,
  And doubly know my blest completeness;
Her lighted eyes, with mine, peer doubly deep,
Catching the full sublimity of things;
  Our words are wedded;
Our touches leap in magnetic marriage;
The dual heart converts the dual will,
  Till it be quick to harmony;
And by the spirit's language do we worship
And every sense bespeaks the silent God.

I know no being mightier than this,
  Loving, and being loved;
For it woos forth all grossness from our lives,
  And sanctifies them unto golden truth;
It is the link between myself and kind—
  This woman-worshiping—
A covenant between my Lord and me,
That, charm-like, draws me heavenward.

Most happy I, when having most of love,
  And I have most of love when I love most;
It is the truth that shall redeem the world—
  Possession in proportion as we give,
  Enlightenment as we enlighten,
  Salvation in the ratio that we save,
The soul's own compensation in its works—
  The key to blissful immortality!

And, Oh, confide with ample confidence;
   Thy trust is darling as my eye's pupil,
   And sacred as the chamber of my God!
True unto thee is true unto myself,
And th' divine majesty of my light,
     That cannot lead astray;
Thy faith shall make thee whole as Beauty is,
And lead thy soul, through me, to happiness,
   And Love's exalted adorations.


Never, my soul-wife, can I let thee go,
For I have tasted of thy sweet infinity,
And felt the delicious burnings of thy breath
     Baptise me unto ecstasy!
Thy warm life floods me with its spell
     Like a new sun!
   And in its potent emanations,
I find the sacred ravishments of time,
And know the blessedness of sweet content.


Were I to lose thee, fair Creatress,
   Then would I understand decay,
   And the cold ways of barren famine;
I think it better that I had not been . .
   Else fashioned for no other thing
Than the mere jest and minute-toy of Fate!
   What though with fertile sorrows
I irrigate the desert left to me,
Yet whence the warmth and pregnant light
To woo one blank oasis into bloom,
   Even of a grave's measurement?
Nay, thou fount of all my Nile of life,
I must have thee and partake of thee,

As thou wert the very end of things,
   Or key to where no end can be!
And I will hold thee by Love's chains
   That fasten where thy soul is deepest;
And by Devotion's singleness,
   That charms thee heaviest
   With incense of its altars,
Till we are inter-wed like wine floods,
   And have but one identity!


O, slay me with thy kisses' scythe, beloved;
   Thy kisses that are warm and heavenly moist,
   Conveying vintages more stinging sweet,
Than all th' distilled flowers of mother Earth!
Thy presence, mine, is quick with joyousness,
   And th' weird prophecies of the Infinite!


There is no marvel that I cling to thee,
   And have thee to my finger-tips;
My consciousness is full of thee,
   Unto my soul's fastnesses;
Thou art a shrine frieghted with miracles,
   And he must yield who would be God-bound!
Thou art my bearer of the lighted Truth;
   For the Beautiful has set us free,
And the heart conveys the head to majesty,
   And Arcana of exalted happiness.


Pr'y thee, beloved, be not too near to me;
   Thy touch is keen as lightning's knife,
That cleaves the pale heart of night,
   And leaves it trembling in wild wonderment;
Even the soft tinseling thou wear'st,

Is instinct with strange quickness;
Like spirit feet upon thin brittle glass,
In telegraphy to its soul—to break!

. . .

The ring, see, has cut clean to th' bone!
So these pregnant flowers thou gavest me,
   Taught by thy vital breath to breathe,
Thou knowest not they burn and scald like fire. .
   Howbeit their color is of blood—*my* blood!

. . . . .

Thy presence is a perfume, lovely thing,
   And when thou sighest with thy tender soul,
Or sham'st the diamond with thy jewel tear,
   Thou fill'st the world with thy crushed fragrance,
And I smell thy sacred sweetness to my depths!
Thy breath's dews are as spirit wine,
And I drink thee—sharper than gods' armita,
   'Till I'm renewed by angel healing,
And praise my God, through thee, for my sublimity!
Or speak—and a fountain stream tinkling
   O'er stalagma is thy music speech,
And beautiful as the path of the white fawn
   Traced out by sun-lit flowers;
And I am as thou'lt have me; thy tongue's convert,
   And convert of thine eyes I am;
And I yield unto thy eloquence with worship!
   Crying amen—and yet amen—to thee!

\* \* \* \* \*

Great souls love not as the low orders love;
   Brute life is true to its developement,
   Be so the higher Mind to his;

And let the emanations from Manhood,
   In deed and word and presence,
Be noble as God's seal within it set,
   **And** mirror forth the everlasting light!

## THE MUSE HUMANITY

The unctious brotherhood of men, O sing,
   And music forth the trumpets of good will;
The universal bliss attunes the string,
   A new Muse hymns from forth the Sacred Hill.

The later muse Humanity—more bright,
   More burning fair and wondrous with sweet grace,
Than any yet born of the womb of Light,
   With laughing love enraptured in her face.

Lo, a still voice soothes the troubled breast,
   And calms the frigid torment of the brain:
Poor hands aweary find the wand of Rest,
   And dying Hope new cause to live again!

For gentle Love sits on the throne of Might,
   A noble Pride stands forth where Shame has stood,
The blind rejoice that they have found new sight,
   The selfish that they found their fellows' good.

O, muse last singing from the patient skies,
   The pris'ners' friend and friend of the oppressed,
Show willful man the cunning to be wise,
   And bleeding man the pathway to be blest.

Break thou, fierce Joy, the leaden veil of care,
   For righteous judgments rule the race of man!
The Curse has learned the milder voice of prayer,
   Salvation found a far diviner plan!

## VENUS URANIA

Sweet Lord, thy Daughter!
   The radiant gift of all thy gifts concentred. .
Thou knewest well, O, deeply visioned Sire,
There must be *cause* for Worship and for Joy,
   And the fair motion of the steps of time!—

For things stood death-still waiting for a sign. .
   Some revelation to be wondered forth,
   That would make chaos blossom and be glad. .
And lo, Necessity is clothed with Beauty!
   And Being with unheard-of Eloquence,
Raining sweet unction on the naked Earth!
   Now are the heavens wide ope'd
     By fingers freighted with the sweet of life,
   And the quick story of our bliss revealed. .
The fair skies are fairer for her light,
The wan stars for her illumination—
   And th' untried pulsations of young Time,
Winged on the purple couriers of Love,
Have caught the shining magic of her smile,
   And to earth gave a priceless legacy.

Now, Joy, thou hast sweet cause in all thy veins!
   Rebound thou over the enchanted hills,
And trip elastic to Orion's arms. .
   Yea, thou shalt dance with moon-beams, thou,
And twirl thy snow-hair about Caucasus!
   And kiss at will the curled lips of the sea!

Or thou shalt wake the sleeping shells to song. . '
  The scallop chambers of all voices
  Poised with the eternal harmonies. .
All bird-carolings and minstrelsies of ocean,
  Wind-melodies and pæans of the pines,
  Attuned like lovers fluted tongues—
All whisperings of the soft-lipped spheres,
  The star-Nine—nine million-fold—
In chorus that re-echoes through the worlds!

And lo, in this sweet odorous name—
  White-browed Urania—
Man may perceive the temper of thanksgiving,
Soul moved to holiest adorations. . .
That the black Earth is green and golden:
  The lead sky lighted as with quicksilver:
  The cold Sea warmed to gladness:
That the tyrannic Seasons as they roll
  Are the dear painters of our varied selves
  Missioning for the unity of joy;
That Darkness is a shell illumed within,
  Awaiting to become some hero's glory:
That all slight things are yet unripened fruit,
  Infected with the everlasting Good,
Time-blessed with benedictions for Eternity.
Now, Lord, I see how very fair thou art!
  How bright thy brightness is—
How warm the warmth of thine eye-lighted sun!
Thine eloquence burns heartward with its sweet,
  And trembles o'er the soul-strings,
  As o'er yon tremulous leaves
The re-flex of the nervous-lighted sea;

And I know how in thou art God's minister
    For noble works—
    Supremest Wonder—
Heaven sent to show the splendid Joy of Things.

Sweet Lord, thy Daughter!
She the type of thy perfectest grace,
    Moulded in thy loveliest sweet moment:
    Lord *she* is the savior to most men!—
    For by her all men prove they love thee
    And justify thy ways to human kind!

# IN MEMORIAM

HENRY WADSWORTH LONGFELLOW—BORN 1807. DIED 1882.

    O ears, ye cannot hear aright!
      Or has Death struck the voices mute
      That once stole from a honeyed flute,
    Like couriers of vocal light
    Poised in immortal flight?

Howbeit the chiselled furrows of Time's streams
Cut deep their resolute wills, then break apace,
And fade like very water from the face
Of things that die . . . . the clay that maketh dreams
    Makes fissures for Time's streams.

But the soul's whisperings are create of stuff
Less tamely brittle to be worn hard down . .
And there are architects, or smile, or frown,
To mar whose works earth has not fire enough—
    Made of such living stuff.

And where his muse's finger touched my life
Or its sweet story clove across glad eyes
In the divine engraving of the skies
Soul-prints are cut nowhere in Nature rife,
    Outliving Nature's life.

Or where one faltered in the weary hours,
There new force came and light for all dark ways . .
A lifted eyelid lifted up lost days,
And unborn hope and heavenly-quickened powers
    Awoke from weary hours.

A wondrous message calm as Luna's light,
The savor of all scented sweets it had,
The incense-breath of flowers young and glad,
Strange fascinations that invoked the sight .
    To fill it with new light.

Symboling the reward of things, and joy,
And that for which men live and suffer pain,
Bared unto fire and storm and night and rain
Of danger, toying with trouble as a toy,
    Because of this sweet joy.

Yea, charmed feet have traced the better way,
And led Life forth—the Muse of Energy;
Howe'er may that be lost whose ministry
Is woven in the fibers of your day
    Each step of all the way?

Whose fair ambitious pinnacles look through
To the fine upper air, and columned face,
Sculptured with glad curves of noble grace,
Alight with wisdom, visioned with the true,
    Peers the whole heavens through.

Delighting in the wide sweet ways of heaven
As stars in the sun's light; and full of pride,
That flowers of good deeds bloom on either side;
To him who gives bright gifts brighter is given
    At the wide hands of heaven.

That forgets not where once the eye looked love,
Or the tongue spake some good thing with its might,
Or the feet led one waif from out the night,
Or a hand's pressure that was parcel of
    A soul invoked by love.

That babbles not unto the noisy throng
Ear-full of shallowness, but speaks full low
The heavenly-nurtured bliss that it does know,
Gladlier than the glamour of a song
    Caught from some spirit throng.

I well know thou art not dead—nor *can* die;
The spirit's good—*that* is the thing that lives
With fierce tenacity; the grace it gives
Tuned to the shining harmonies on high
    Will learn not how to die.

The soul shall from its baser ashes rise
As chrysalid from its gold sheath outgrown,
Or Hope forth from Pandora's prison flown,
Delivered from Life's sackcloth to the skies
    Where the real self may rise.

And thy great song knew how to search God out!
Pricking to worship true each dumb dead sense,
And binding it with deep Omnipotence;
Aye, bound the soul's soul with a cordage stout,
    Searching the good God out.

Making life worthful and most wondrous sweet,
Pregnant with great, glad purposes, with use,
Born of truth's truth and not of her abuse;
Hail to the upturned face and winged feet
    Moved by a muse most sweet;

Tripping upon the lifted edge of Sea;
Or like Camilla with inspired bound,
Scarce bending the grain's beard on the light round
Of darling duty, young and wildly free,
    Quicker than the edge of Sea!

And thy song's good is rooted fast; as 'bides
The brown stain of a lion's eye to life,
Or Sol's warm breath to whom he takes to wife;—
Yea, when the Sun-lord slays his starry brides,
  The good of thee abides.

And crowns men with the laurel of sweet grace,
The love of all things cherished by thy love;
Strange exaltations and adorings wove
By threads of thee in beauty of God's face,
  And glory of his grace.

# THE CHANGES OF THE SHELL

Whilom I struck the changes of my shell,
　The soul strings of a varied instrument,
　To me and to all willing list'ners lent—
And gathered thus the accents as they fell.

### FIRST CHANGE—FREEDOM

Responsible, immortal Choice,
　One with the Disposer, Will,
　　Choice that is proud, Self-hood's voice,
　　Will whose tongue cannot be still,
　　Joyous that it *can* rejoice—
O, privilege of weal or woe,
　O, freedom born with birth of life,
O, death to die, O, growth to grow,
　Desire that is the darling strife . . .
Let men pursue the loves and hates,
　The pains and pleasures as they fly,
The truths and lies that Time relates,
　And dare the boasts of destiny.

### SECOND CHANGE—WISDOM

The wake that traverses the dark,
　And hisses through the sullen gloom—
　　Dark that hath no single spark,
　　Gloom whose kinship is the tomb,
　　And no thing to prove an ark—
Now shall the passage be of light,

Now Understanding lead the way,
  One thing can cleave the mask of night,
    And bid its barrenness be day,
Convert sweet Peace to be a guest,
  Give Pain the summons to depart,
Show weariness the place of rest,
  And happiness the troubled heart.

### THIRD CHANGE—TRUTH

The Truth of one that is a Lie
  When issued from another's brain—
    Lie because it did not cry
    "Train me to a riper strain,
    Teach me to arise and fly ". .
That thing which is a growth replete,
  The stature of a word or deed,
The sweetness of a life when sweet,
  The blood that's given it to bleed,
The Whole that cannot beg nor lend,
  Ripened fruit of earth and space,
Perfection of an act or end,
  And very head-light of the race.

### FOURTH CHANGE—VIRTUE

Virtue—that is the child of Truth,
  And of whom Wisdom is the sire—
    Truth that is perennial youth,
    Fire that is not made of ire,
    That slays the canker and the tooth—
O, Strength where weakness would have been,
  O, Health where lean decay had clung,

Teach aspiration how to win,
  And youth the cunning to be young,
Discover with thy sober charm
  The triumphs of the passing hour,
That Vigilance which conquers harm,
  That Temperance whose name is Power.

### FIFTH CHANGE—BEAUTY

Th' divine Form and Grace of things,
  And th' quick soul of grace and form—
    Things to which completion clings,
    Form, O, stronger than the storm,
    Nature's happier offerings—
God saw the reason for this same,
  The proud warm argument of life, .
The inspiration without name,
  The Beauty man would take to wife,
And lo! it fills the earth and air,
  O, sweetness to repletion grown,
O, Woman fairer than aught fair,
  O, all that's charmful to be known.

### SIXTH CHANGE—LOVE

The Love that is the Soul of all,
  And crowning victory of God!
    All—replete as is a ball—
    God because outgrown the rod,
    Glory that outlives the gall—
O, this is that fair Queen of Kings,
  That so well marries heart to heart,

The vital Web that weds all things,
   And makes them to forget to part,
The fullest answer to all prayer,
   The precious universal Leaven,
Reward of ev'ry cross we bear,
   And Substance of immortal Heaven.

## ODE TO COLUMBIA

What splendid thing is the theme
   Of mariners over the sea . . .
Is it fairy enchantment or dream,
Or precious miraculous gleam
   Of a new maiden-savior to be?
But none of all eyes that had seen,
Perceived her full stature or mein . .
Some saw but the sweep of her hair,
As she flashed through the tremulous air,
As she fled like an arrow of fire.
Others caught sounds—as a lyre,
And some heard the one word—*dare*.
One said. . "In the solemn bleak night,
Bound by a tyrannous fright,
Her hand grappled hold of the reins,
And loosed ev'ry chain of our chains!"
Then said another, aghast,
"Deep in the deep sea's waste,
When by the wild skies tossed
Ocean cried out as if lost!
I saw this same wonderful form
Borne in the arms of the storm,
And laugh with a shrill thrilling glee
Over wrath of the sky and the sea."

Howbeit some ships sailing West
   With faint and irresolute helm

And doubts that did nigh overwhelm,
'Mid blank barren searchings for Rest . .
Saw this Token flash forth from the sky,
And without asking whither nor why—
Since surely a Pilot was given
As the Sign of the pleasure of Heaven—
Strained on like glad hounds through the deep
In the wake of the star-lighted leap.

And she led them—this Pilot of Peace—
To Liberty's land of release,
  Where heel never smote the free soul . .
Or daring to type its foul tread,
Had died with the things that are dead,
  Or blended with death in the scroll
That Life had since worshiped and wed
  And won to immortal control.

And lo, everywhere! everywhere!
  Upon the magniloquent shore,
  With its boiling and coiling and roar
Upon the weird wings of the air,
Afar on the precipice bare,
Or near on the rock-broken sod,
  This presence discovered her trace
  Like a smile from a heavenly face,
As the land were her darling abode;
And secure in a Genius of might,
In a Guardian-Goddess-of-Light,
The band grappled hard to the strife
That prophesied Glory and Life!

Ah, now shall these build a race
   And parent the New World's plains?
Aye, fearling, these same by the grace
   Of the red sterling health in their veins,
And the force that is writ in their face . . .
There are, among Earth's mankind,
Some souls that a chain cannot bind . . .
Some souls so untempted by pelf,
Some heroes so emptied of self,
That they break from their lives' narrow pen
And dare a new blessing for men,
Nor query what part *they* will share
If hap'ly they do what they dare.

---

Such were the Spartan-bred few,
Inspired with the gift to be true,
   And waiting the gift to be free,
Here armed in the House of the Blue
   In common with Sea and with Sea.

One morning—some fierce days after—
With joy and merry sweet laughter,
The sun—and with wandering ken—
Beheld this new order of men,
And the work their strong hands found to do:
'Twas a sight most impressive to view . .
They had dragged the wild brute from his lair
   And taught him to crouch at their feet;
They had torn up the rocks black and bare,
   And planted their furrows with wheat;
They converted the tortuous coasts
   To havens of smooth sure rest;
Had driven the red forest hosts
   To the arms of the infinite West;

On the breasts of the young Thirteen,
Strange charms and new graces were seen—
The wilderness fled with the wind,
And the beautiful sovereignty—Mind—
Succeeded the reign of the Night
With auroras of love and of light.

We will see now what people is this,
   Whether made of the earth or the sky—
   The hours came forth with a cry
That was born in Oppression's abyss ..
"Lo, here is a yoke for your neck—
That till now hath no sign of a fleck—
Here are some gyves for your feet,
And here some fresh wormwood to eat:
They were typed and made at the forge
That is Kinged by the English George,
And here are his lictors in red,
Sent to order the work of his head,
And cunning wrought out by his hand,
Through the height and the depth of your land!

Then ten-thousand voices as one
Made reply to this thing that was done ..
"We are men that for conscience' sake
Were compelled to give o'er and to break
With the whole painted love of the world;
In dear Freedom's name we were hurled
Upon Ocean's tumultuous breast
To this gem of hers shrined in the West;
But we found on the rough welcome coast
The delights that our bosoms love most;
Found in forests fresh-scented and wild,
In mountains of strength newly piled,

In sweets of a generous soil,
In the health and the culture of toil,
With none to molest or annoy,
A peace and contentment and joy,
We never had tasted before,
Nor dreamed it were even in store.

"No man have we wronged in this thing,
Neither Bishop nor Sultan nor King;
We withdrew from the light of the throne,
And rather chose darkness alone;
To find out in silence, apart,
The tie 'twixt our God and our heart.

"Think not we will suffer again
The meanness and danger of men;
We have learned to obey and deny,
We have learned, too, to live and to die!
We've forgot to be mute in our choice,
Our virtues now speak in our voice,
O, pure and sonorous and free,
As the story that leaps from the sea!

"We will yield not this fill of our needs,
This asylum of ours and our seeds,
To any that live while we live!
Self-truth is no gift we can give,
And no Master in all of Life's van
Is so great as a self-mastered Man,
Or fitter to rule his own charge,
Though e'en he were Three times a George."

Herewith were these Pioneers smote—
And from many a brown lusty throat

That late made its honest acclaim,
There issued a red liquid flame,
That like Ætna a-leaping on high,
Told its story to earth and to sky,
And stirred the whole sensitive land;
And lo, it arose heart in hand,
'Rose from hiltop and valley and plain,
Quick with courage and muscle and brain,
Unmindful of station or caste,
Singly fired by the present and past,
Singly bent on defeating a fate
That was kindred to Hell and to Hate!

Ah, now, what a day was begun
With thy red dawn, O, brave Lexington—
It needs was a miracle-morn
That saw a Republican born
Who would challenge the crowns of all Earth!
A day with a gory fierce girth,
Whose moments were battles of pain,
Each breaking a link of a chain!

No Patriot tardy or lax
  In the glorious work to be done;
When an ag-ed one fell in his tracks
  His place was re-filled by his son;
In the homestead, or hamlet, or hall,
  Firm women did other than toy,
The wife armed her husband, her all,
  The mother her brave only boy!

Oh, the struggle unequal and long,
Where weakness finds out it is strong;

In the name of a solemn sweet cause,
These few dare the iron awful jaws
Of an Hydra—to slay or be slain;
Every nerve is put forth to the strain,
With a resolute spiriting trust,
That triumph was true to the just,
And giants of sucklings are made
When Right crieth upward for aid.

\* \* \* \* \* \*

O, vain to oppose, O despair!
　When there is that in the air
That maketh heroes of the very dead!
　The dead that die unto life,
　That take sweet Victory to wife,
Becoming glorious in the thing they wed.

As for the quick, lo, here is Washington!
With his brave hand a thousand years upon,
Standing as that stands which is a Sun.

Melt ye the rock-hills into waters blue,
Or stay the eternal tear-drops of white dew,
Or hide the colors of the warm sky's smile;
　But think ye not meanwhile
To cleave or quench or kill this spirit born,
Or make Night pall the genius of this Morn,
Cutting Man off from all of him that's true.

　For Man so moved apace,
And filled with God-hood to the burning brim,
　Will sicken and wear out stupendous space,
Appall Olympus with the ghost of him,
　Forgetting not to vivify his place.

I see now that Triumph must be,
    Nay that he *is*
    With all Columbia his,
Wrested from the torment of the sea ..
And the prairies cry, *it was our prophecy!*
And the lakes reply, *it was our ministry!*
And Freedom sings, *it is my Glory!*

   \*    \*    \*    \*    \*    \*

Hail to this thing that is born!
Hail to the Herald of morn!
All hail unto her who hath borne
The darlingest gem Time hath worn
In the innermost shrine of his heart!
Oh, stay! thou and we cannot part!
Art thou not crowned as with light,
Thy forehead star-jeweled and white,
Are not many balms in thy breast,
Thine arms full of rapture and rest,
Who fitter than thou for a wife,
That art the Aurora of life?

And now adown the current of glad years,
Aglow and wonderful as a comet's train,
    The new great race appears!
The steam-horse plows the everlasting plain,
    And golden lusty grain
Doth wave beside the mountains' golden tears.

And, lo, a splendid Mind-burst spreads its light
  O'er the immortal Monarchy of Man—
    The sober, lawful privilege began
To solve the sacred mystery of Might,
    And make it clean and white.

# A LAMENT FOR CHILDE HAROLD

## I

Hark to yon lyre's converting strains of bliss,
Sweetly magnetic as from silver spheres,
Descending from their world to hallow this,
And wake the glad hosannas of the years;
But lo! what hopes are stayed by waking fears,
That climb discordant upon guilty bars,
Harshness intrusive, which that same world bears?
'Tis some rich sea whose song its own wrath mars,
Or vocal clouds of night fast raining from the stars.

## II

Forsooth there are whose thought is like a kite,
That soars a given string and never higher;
Who mask the broad immensities of sight,
Or vainly burn the ashes of desire;
They are dumb slaves, for who dares not aspire
To the poor verge of star-worlds and their lore,
Is held in darkness, hid in mental mire,
A stumbling mishap in Progression's door,
Self-exiled from himself and Life's most precious store.

### III

Not such thy proud lot, Singer of the Sea!
Thy mind partook of that thy wild lyre sung—
The boundless nature of the brave and free,
The summer-time of being strong and young ..
And so did live its fellow-minds among,
A quick fierce thing whose flights were never stayed
By cell nor fetter, but whose weird tongue
Baptised its music in a fire far made,
Or like an numbered Nile o'erswept where'er it swayed.

### IV

Strange types of men Parnassus has surveyed,
But none have stirred a more profounder sense
Of pleasure pierced with pain than was conveyed
By this Childe Harold; the shining excellence
That marked the man; the bold magnificence
With which his tale was told; his feelings fine,
And his torn passions, fertile and intense,
Did each and all their earnest pleas combine
To prove him but part clay still fired by the divine.

### V

But that worst part was of the dregs of gall!
Oh, what extreme conditions may possess
Mysterious man! nothing at once, and all!
Angel and fiend, god-slave, a wilderness
Of strewn spent mightiness, a force to bless
And curse at will—and such the problem Childe—
Rising and falling with a proud distress—
Now a glad summer by soft suns beguiled,
Now night, Oh, trebly dark and chaos rent and wild.

## VI

Hast thou, Apollo, ever known a son
So strong at once and weak, whose sky-brought fire
Was speeded out ere half his day was done?
Aye, one; that strange self-tortured slave, whose lyre
Was frenzy's toy—Rousseau—he to admire
Must love, and loving rave, and raving mould,
Convert, lead captive by his splendid ire!
Both like, yet all unlike; the one a bold,
Bright comet was—the last a molten stream of gold.

## VII

He stood alone, a child of pain and passion!
Kin to the storm-god, and dark forests, and the sea,
And flowers of night; for a less strange relation
Was beneath his soul, and others died where he
Drank with a wild thirst this awful mystery,
Fatting upon the draught. Nay, not alone!
All restive things were of his company;
The insane roots had mixed in him and grown,
'Till he was re-create and statured bone by bone.

## VIII

His life was but a tragedy—enacted,
As are most such 'mid diamonds and dust,
Delights and death; and while not protracted
Closed doubly unfulfilled; nor by the thrust
Of want or eating care, nor the chill *must*
Di-ease deliberates was he subdued,
But by the affection's war, the fierce lust
That woos satiety and her sickening brood,
A sacrifice self-slain amid a self-sought feud.

## IX

Yet far with him has many a lover strayed,
And drank with him deep draughts from Beauty's well,
And joyed with him all that his joy essayed,
And mourned with him when blight that joy befell,
Until he yearned to live the darling spell,
And linger alway at the varied feast—
Dear Art's and dearer Nature's festival—
Nor would he from such summer be released,
Nor further unction ask of either prince or priest.

## X

And such have been who more than all beside
Loved this unstaid creation—this dark light—
Most wondrously; for 'twas to them a bride
Unsexed and wedded by the soul's warm rite,
And shrined within the soul from common sight;
Beloved the more, not for its waywardness,
But that this wooed forgiveness, wherein right
Is most righteous, and does most impress,
And woo in turn Love's heart, which wooing is to bless.

## XI

And with this sense and sympathy most sweet,
Many a swain his being bade to grow;
'T is youth echoed in youth; warm spring replete
With spring's fresh fountains and unebbing flow
Of beaming bursting life; none, none, may know
So well as youth the all that youth endures,
For age forgets its morning and its glow,
The season of young loves and young allures;
And that sufficient red oft crushing while it cures.

## XII

Between glad hopes and bitter memories,
There is a fitful yet immeasured space
Deep as thought is.  Stern facts and fallacies
Strain their last sinews in the telling race,
And the victor finds him on the top-most place,
Or else the least: so one is youthful spring,
Leaping with his red quick pulses in the chase,
The other, winter—a spent, tired, barren thing,
That mocks with his dumb mouth and pierces with his sting.

## XIII

There is a grand necessity in living,
Without which life were emptiness—distress;
A dream most troubled and a toy, giving
Perchance amusement but not happiness,
Naught that can truly charm or surely bless;
But in this stern and unescapable must
Dwells that which gives taste, tone and measureless
Impulse to our being—warming the dust
That else would chill and clog and curse with sluggish rust.

## XIV

So Life is not the chapter of a spell,
The hollow sound and shadow of a thing,
Else why does it unto the heaven's swell,
And from a thousand worlds, their secrets wring,
And unto them its potent fire-pulse fling,
Search the sea depths and secrecies of space,
Fill nature with its quick inhabiting,
Infinitude loud challenge in its race,
And e'en o'er vanquished Death assert its pregnant place?

## XV

Aye! turn from yonder rabble's noisy store!
For gold, not glory, fills them; the dead weight
Of covetous to-day, corpse-like, hangs o'er
Man-forms ordained for worthier freight;
No marvel thou dost sicken in this state,
This strata of disease and hungry dearth,
Mirage of night and dust insatiate;
Thou art a stranger to their earthy earth,
Who without human weal, would measure human worth.

## XVI

So let them hiss and hate thy hatefulness!
Their own is greater who conceal their sin,
And falsely great, brand others vilely less;
Let none unjudged too proudly judge; for in
This world, this labyrinth of life, we scarce begin
Our errand ere we pause—pause but to err,
To wrestle with uncertainty and din,
And darkness, then distress; life's fledgling stir
Woos foreign aid, the last as well a minister.

## XVII

And they do crown poor vanity who cry,
"I am more holy, brother worm, than thou,"
Where all are wanting in truth's constancy . .
Expel the beam from 'neath thine own dark brow,
That better thou may'st teach thy betters how;
Let thy reviler's shout, unclean, lose sound
For very shame. Ah, could all men but bow
Like Nazareth to Right's most royal round,
None, none, would cast the stone which their own flesh would wound.

## XVIII

Yea, turn, to Nature's tongues and be as they,
Young with the beauty of fair life, and glad
With sweet repose of power; what they essay
Is the soul's paradise of peace: O, had
You stay'd and drank, poor heart, ere in a mad
Maturity you thirsted for such drink,
With scarce a sense to find, it far less sad
Had been your fate; and far less would you shrink
From life wherein you lie a lame, unwilling link.

## XIX

Yet shall thy blood-tears purge thy travailed soul,
And life's strong chastisement and bitter-sweet,
Baptise and re-create thee: thy proud goal
Shall be a strange thanksgiving all replete,
With an all-conquering love; when thy strayed feet—
Forgetful of their pilgrimage of fire—
Shall stand truth-tried; and thy great self shall greet
The source of greatness where each proud desire
Shall covet Wisdom's wealth and mount forever higher.

## THY NAKED FEET

Sitting by thy naked feet,
  Farinella, lovely thing,
  Magical emotions spring,
Filling th' fonts of life replete—
  Sitting by thy feet.

Worshiping two marble feet,
  Streaked with tiny truant veins,
  Purple, pretty, precious stains,
Let time be less cruel fleet—
  Worshiping thy feet.

Holding two white fairy feet,
  How oft the couriers of joy,
  Bearers of laughter, chaste and coy,
Let Pleasure pipe an homage meet—
  Holding fairy feet.

Loving slight and tender feet,
  Carved like ivory keys to thrill,
  Brain and breast alike they fill,
Heart of hearts with raptures beat—
  Loving tender feet.

Petting pink and lily feet,
   Soft and warm and closely pressed,
   Deep their lover's dear unrest,
White round ankles peep and greet—
   Petting lily feet.

Caressing both thy velvet feet,
   Drinking blisses warm with sighs,
   Bound beneath seducing eyes,
Love! prolong this heaven sweet—
   Caressing velvet feet.

## THE GARDEN OF THE SEA

### A REVERY ON THE BIRTH OF CALIFORNIA

Once when the stars in wonderment stood still,
And from Sierra's crest the plumes of night
By torches of red flame were cleft, and down
Fierce slopes the lava-dragon crept hissing
To his watery lair, hidden and deep,
Lo, Sea's vast travail stormed again; as when
In earlier wrath, fire-armored and severe,
She carved the Himalayas of the West,
And bade them awe the land!

          Dawn came! and lo!
Upon the horizon dim the tragedy
Of a later Coast had been! now calm in
Titan majesty.  Pacific's main a
New shore lashed, yet warm with heat of conflict:
Between—still kissing the Sierra's feet—
A shallow sea, pearl-breasted and serene,
Lay like a liquid dream.

          And like a dream
The panorama of its being passed.
Adown the slopes quick streams of molten rock

Poured ceaselessly, fringing the sea about
With vesturings of steam, ghostly and wan,
While mid-sea, too, white vapor-fountains rose,
Climbed the swift clouds and then rained back again.

But when night came, black-browed and terrible,
Came also sights to marvel at. The Sea's
Breast with fiery nipples flashed and burned;
Now high in air, now low in terraces
Of iridescent flame; now, above all,
Shafts of slender red bursting at the top,
In blossoms of pale blue, and sheafs of light,
Illumed the purple lawns and tinged with soft
And vari-colored tones the vapory plumes.
Anon, red bubbles on the troubled waste,
Chased one another to some sudden gap,
Where now in lofty wonder rose a vast
Portiere of fluid earth, festooned and arched,
And livid with metallic light. Above
The burning flora mountain craters burned:
On either side, Coast-wise and Sierra,
The very hills had life and the stern crags
Swayed in a passionate torment. Afar,
Red tongues the lowering cloudlets lapped;
And torches, fierce with fiery agony,
Lit the mute realm.

Upon the noiseless pinion
Of young Time strange chances came. Fire-flowers
For flowers of frost were changed, and the Ice-god
Dominion held o'er the lame Lemnian's
Forges of red woe. 'Twas but a different
Violence; for soon with scimeter keen
The Frost-king smote, splintering the crags,
And cañons yawned where ploughed the avalanche.

What metamorphosis befell the Sea?
Fire, ice, the storm and torrent ceased them not—
While years sped lazily like drifting sands
Upon the bosom of this lessening waste—
'Til it was Sea no more! All elements
Made it the garden of their jubilee.
Isles and moraines, all-sized and vari-shaped,
Rose from the weary waters and outspread
Erewhile, to join the ever narrowing shore.
New forces came, lightning and the northern blast,
And from rent aiguilles the torrent leaps
With thunderous laugh, sundering the hills,
And headlong gathering the mountain streams,
Bears their black fruitage to the lowland waste.
With rumbling tread the glacier stalks abroad,
Moulding the valley slopes and sculpturing forth
The pathway of the rivers of the plain.

What thing sublimely cradled thus has come
Of all these wondrous alchemies and forms?
From chain to chain a radiant land now sweeps,
With swells as gentle as the ancient sea,
And flowered as fair. But lava-leaves and rods
Of flame and plumages of vapory
Flora, magical with dainty colorings,
For the red rose is changed and fruited vine;
And for the Sea's soft green, stretches of grass;
While patient grazing herds now shade and dot
The drowsy undulations of the downs.
From snow-clad crests slight streams leap down the l
Of mountain cañons and glide forth gladly,
Watering the plain. Bright yellow grain is here;
Orchards purple, mauve and russet with rich stores;

While moss-grown pines climb the gradual slopes
And sweep in forests that astound the earth!
This is the thing that Sea and Fire have wrought—
Fair California with her golden fruit,
The Garden of the New Hesperides!

## GLORIA MILITAIRE

Ah, me, if thine own hand, perchance,
    Should slay thee, France,
Ma belle! Ma belle! the fairest of the brides,
    Put out thy great glad eyes,
    Light-bearers of the skies,
And spill thy scented red upon the tides—
Who would bear on the guerdon of thy glance
    When thou art dead, sweet France?

The knife that brings keen tears to start
    Forth from the heart—
Ma belle! Ma belle! put thou it by, forsooth,
    The white-flamed tongue of hell,
    That tells thy mocking knell,
As of one cut death-wise in th' dream of youth—
Where stands he who would work thy wondrous part
    If thou wert dead, dear heart?

No dagger will begirt the side
    Of Earth's true Bride—
Ma belle! Ma belle! disarm before too late,
    And spurn the hardihood,
    Whose valor is in blood,
The false, red lie of an ignoble fate . .
Else how can we the stricken night abide
    When we have lost our Bride?

The spent, torn toys of childhood's play,
> Man puts away—
Ma belle! Ma belle! thou seemest ripe and fair,
> Thy neck curled like the sea,
> And thy feet wondrously
A-nestle 'neath hewn meshes of bright hair—
How shall Time know that Earth has reached her May,
> When thou hast fled away?

## "COME!"

Above all sounds of the eloquent earth,
  A cry smote my ear
Like a rose's cry as it springs to birth,
One slight wild word, but a heaven of cheer,
A lisp that conveyed all the songs of a year—
  "Come!"

To that which in one is your white, red and blue,
  All below, all above,
To the Augusta and Lucia of you,
To the bosom all burdens of balm are of,
To her your embrace and your soul of love—
  "Come!"

If joy be sought by your staggering feet,
  Or bliss be your quest,
If you yearn to discover the sweets that are sweet,
If eager to find out the way that is best,
If weary in search of the jewel of rest—
  "Come!"

## MEMORIA IN ETERNA

Yea, passion can be still as very Death!
   Or as a frighted god stand fixed and white . .
   But in the depths of it there is a might
That like old Ocean's soul can hold its breath—
      All still as very Death!

When the bright colors of the grass are lost,
   Or from the serpent's side the stripes are bleached,
   Remembrance having thus far fully reached
May falter with the burden it held most—
      When the Earth's green is lost!

For some sweet things scar deep into the soul,
   As well he knows who whilom held Love's hand . .
   And like a Cain thenceforward wore a brand
That typed Love's story on his being's scroll—
      Well cut into the soul!

O, wondrous record from the fair new Sea
   More wildly sweet than Sinai! ah, God!
   There are who say thy other name is Good . .
And *she* is that best good and grace to me,
      Thou gavest from the sea!

For she did move the motion of my life
  With force that fails not . . taking sweet deep root
  Within the soul-pulse and with noiseless foot
Searched the dead depths of me—now quick and rife
  With new undying life.

O, Joy! quicker than fire! O, Hope of things!
  O, gracious gladness mighty with delight!
  O, subtle sweet, delightfuler than might!
Ah, me, no fiercer laughing unction springs
  From the fair Hope of things!

The keenly-chiseled foot-prints of wan Time
  Are deep enough . . full deep the maelstrom nests,
  The dark incisions 'twixt the mountain breasts,
Grief-lines that pierced our common Mother's prime,
  And seamed the face of Time:

And this were true, what of the circling arms
  That dammed th' enamored currents of the throat,
  Palsied as a white snake's folds had smote . .
A first and last dumb sepulchre of charms—
  Deep beneath circling arms!

What of her speech, alas, forged with white fire!
  The tongue's soft tremor or the eyes' sweet stream—
  A dream of language stranger than a dream—
A wing-ed sense as subtle as desire,
  Twin-born with keen white fire!

Upon her shoulders light couched low in sleep . .
  But her mouth's curl was quick with a red kiss,
  Clean as the lips' breath of chaste Artemis,
That scarce had drawn a sigh from Love's dear deep—
  Unwaked from virgin sleep.

Or where some yellow shreds of hair were blown
   Across the languid prisons of the eyes . .
   The light that has fulfilled its uses dies,
And a new sense charms forth since that has flown —
     Where shreds of hair were blown!

Ah, Yolonde of the sunny heart! Ma Belle!
   Thine was the quick god-breath by which I am . .
   That from white silence dead conjured a psalm
Of life—miracle of thy potent spell—
     O, mighty heart! Ma Belle!

One may forget to hunger and to thirst,
   But not the torment where the fierce lip clung,
   The grape whence the last sacrament was wrung
That could renew a spirit when accurst—
     And prompt immortal thirst !

Yea, passion can be still as very Death !
   Or as a frighted god stand fixed and white . .
   But in the depths of it there is a might
That like old Ocean's soul can hold its breath—
     All still as very Death!

## WALT WHITMAN

### I

Of the sages and singers and sons of the vigorous West,
    Of the great hearted land
That is fiercely athirst for the mightier races of Life,
    One man stood aloof—
A singer and teacher and hero more brave than the rest,
    Whose voice smote the soul
Like the sweet grand alarm of a new sea broke into sound!

### II

There is the marvel—America—forth typed in a man!
    With front like the storm,
And eyes that peer down to the shell covered beds of the seas:
    With shoulders of iron,
That the hung'ring blasts shrink back from as wolves from a fire;
    With limbs keenly knit,
Like the tireless stout shafts that prop up a mountain of beryl;
    And a great sun-like soul
That pours its warm cheer upon deserts that break into flowers!

### III

And this is the same that of babes and of sucklings was taught,
    That the birds and the beasts
And the trees and the eloquent streams conversed with and loved,
    That the heart-beat of men
Awakened and thrilled as a brother was born to the Earth!

## IV

And, lo, where men suffered a new fellow sufferer came,
    And with warm tender hand
Bound up the rent sores and requickened the hope that was dead;
    Or where one fell down
Benighted and spent mid the tortuous gauntlet of life,
    A helper of strength,
With fresh light in his face conducted the wayfarer on.

## V

He stands breast high and heart-bound with all that humanity is:
    From the frail human bud,
To the dark-minded bawd and the prisoner bayed by his faults;
    And gives these strange gifts
Of Courage and Faith and sweet Sympathy warmed in the soul;
    Or if want weighs them down,
While his right hand knows not, his left hand finds good things to do.

## VI

For this is the comrade, the helper, the lover of men:
    And the poet of peace:
Of Good-will, Fraternity, Honor and Love that is great . .
    And the strong numbers roll
Like the tread of the Wind over forests of brotherly pines,
    Or sing out mid the morn
The joyous young song of the Now and the hopeful To Be!

## VII

    O, good bringer of Light!
O, Energy, born of the opulent fire of the skies!

In whose wonderful soul
The birth and the death throes of all things are voiced in their m
You have broken fresh seals,
And new vials brought forth whose contents climb back into hea
Light winged and most glad,
Impregnate with Good and the harmonies married to love!

## FOR WOMAN'S SAKE

As the glad sun upon the expectant earth,
A-sparkle with the lover-smile of heaven,
Bids life come forth in rosy robes of joy,
So dost thou, sweet, reverse the force of sex,
And move me to sublimest sovereignty!
Yea, all the juicy leaves of Hope appear,
As 'twere the jocund time of Spring; the vale
Is quick with song, and to the mountain top
Life is pursued how gladly for thy sake,
Strewn with brave toil and fruitage of fair thought.

Thus is thy sweet will done by strength of thee—
Fair Goddess of the harvest of the earth—
And in the magnet of thy radiant eyes,
The miracle of thy touch swifter than
Quicksilver; lo! the wonder-working—
Fierce as the white heat of stars! that paints
Poor Time with colors of Eternity,
And wakes the tongue to everlasting tune!

## "THROUGH THE RAYS SERENE"

### ON AN INFANT'S DEATH

Through the rays serene of a morning sun,
By heaven blessed and by beauty won,
    A tiny dewdrop fell;
In an acorn cup, a retreat it found,
And the moments sped in a gentle round,
    Above the sparkling cell.

But twilight followed the sinking sun,
And night pursued—its day was done—
    Short was its earth-life breath:
A frost approached with a stealthy bound,
And about the gem his cold arm wound,
    And the change was counted—Death!

## SHASTA

List ye! the monarch-mountains! from their thrones
    That boldly pierce the jeweled vaults of blue,
To the lulled plain below there echo tones
    Of massive minstrelsy. 'T is not for you
Nor me to know them half; yet their rock-bones
    Have converse and an eloquence most true,
And rapturous born with their birth of fire . .
Pause, ye, and list to Nature's magic lyre!

Ambitiously they raise their white brows to
    The sky and stand in majesty: broken
And wild, and vast, and steep, and stern, but true
    To awful order: e'en their frowns betoken
Greatliness, and forest-robed or nude, new,
    Old, convulsed or calm, here is outspoken
Joy that thrills the startled air, and a glee,
That shakes the earth with its fierce comedy.

Unto thy august and commanding heights,
    Thou dome of rocks and monument of power,
Let me my tribute bring: thy mien invites
    Profoundest reverence: not thine to cower,
Nor yield thy might nor yoke thy manhood's rights,
    Nor feel a shudder for the direst hour;
But like a world's guardian thou dost stand,
Force in thy face and strength within thy hand!

## CONTEMPLATION ON THE UXMAL RUINS

Approach and pause—there is a feeling here
That stifles words and half provokes a tear;
That comes abroad with wonder overcast,
And coldly points to a mysterious past;
Like to some jewels rare whose radiant trace
Loud mocks the poor dead fingers they encase,
Or dungeon's gloom that here and there hath won
A stream of light from some far-distant sun—
So these strewn fragments pour their pregnant rays,
And speak of distant worlds and mightier days,
Of vast conditions with their human seas,
Of golden cities and voluptuous ease,
When was the pile that now such sadness wings,
The awe of peoples and the pride of kings.

And such the fall that even nations know,
The gilt of thrones at best a fleeting show;
Thus Life and Death by Time are borne along,
Reactions each of Virtue and of Wrong;
Pause then apace—the place is all a grave;
The sepulchre of sovereign and of slave;
Here pride and state resolve to humble dust
The toys and tools of luxury and lust,
And power that erst could dazzle and dethrone
Resigns its sceptre to a crumbling stone!

Is this the finis then of human might,
And this the fall from man's remotest height,
Proud man, who loves his filmy waifs to flaunt,
Replete with his own littleness and want?
Approach, vain god, and scan this emtpy scroll!
And earthiness behold thy earthy goal,
The consummation of a common lot,
Alike dismembered—and alike forgot!

Ah, this is not the all of human strife,
'Tis but a page, and not the book of life!
Oh! God of Law! we bless thee for the text
That makes this world a preface to the next!
A pilgrimage of one short day and night,
An infant school, a fledgling's trial flight,
Where Sense can catch a taste of Heaven's sea,
And Mind a glimmer of the vast to be,
Yet store each deed and thought from very birth
In the great garner of immortal worth!

## THE WÁSTING OF THE FLOWERS

O, the scented bright flowers by the wayside,
    That smile with the colors of spring;
What slight sunny one is the May-bride,
    And which shall be queen of the king?

O, the rosy, the pink, and the starry,
    The white from the brow of a nun;
Yea, this one was born of a fairy,
    And that of a ray of the sun!

O, quick dewy gems of the morning,
    O, pure as the penitent's tear,
The eye of the fawn has had warning,
    It will lose by comparison here.

O, flowers that have hope and ambition,
    The wish to be won and be wed,
Which life will bring fairest fruition,
    And which bring you Sorrow to bed?
The flower-life hath sweet without measure,
    But knows not its sweet from alloy;
But soul-life hath pain with its pleasure,
    The test and the index of joy.

## MISCELLANEOUS

O, flowers, laughing flowers of the May-time,
   With lips that were posed in a kiss,
That whisper through star-time and day-time
   Some tremulous story of bliss,
Speak now to an ear that will listen,—
   And th' breath-dew was warm and not cold,
The deep eyes did gladden and glisten,
   In the beautiful hope that was told.

So the flowers in great faith chose that being
   Where hate is the balance of love;
Where joy is oft courted while fleeing,
   And the eagle oft wed to the dove;
O, man, thou strong lord of creation,
   What sweet grantest thou weaker powers;
What blessing is in thy relation,
   What guardianship for the flowers?

*Si vertu est méprisée donc laissez nous dormir·*

The cold black earth is strewn with lily-leaves!
        The air with spoils of fern;
What woeful shafts despoil the flower-sheaves,
        And the sweet lives that yearn?
Alas, the wasted buds dislimbed and lorn,
   Their scented hope and fair ambition slain;
Alas, the virgin blooms tear-wrung and torn,
   That seek asylum on the homeless plain!

One bright sweet morn a sweet, bright daisy bloomed,
        Kissing the happy air,
And all the vale that this fair life perfumed,
        Rejoiced it was so fair;

Alas, at eventide the sun went out,
    The place had lost its gem,
No song was on the stifled air about,
    No flower upon the stem!

Mayhap some tender hand transplanted it
    To gladden other skies,
That the sweet summer time its light had lit,
    Might smile for other eyes;
Howbeit, its way is sprinkled with new woe,
    Fair leaves are cast apart,
And Beauty's feet leave red stains as they go,
    Leave cries as from the heart!


*Alieni temporis floris!*

O, cruel hands that tear such tender limbs!
  O, impious hands that desecrate such shrines!
Fair God! help him who robs the life he dims—
  Dims and puts out till it no longer shines—
  Help him who slays and stills the sunny rhymes!

What is the end of marriage—is it this?
  A case of jewels cast upon dead air—
A song hushed death-wise by some Judas' kiss—
  A flower to bury in a savage lair?
Alas, the love-feast and the start of Joy,
  Yea, Love's most heavenly burthen of quick pain,
Alas, the travailed gift, the living toy,
  A light of life but lighted to be slain!

Yet nurtured with unspoken tenderness,
  A slight, frail flower nested amid flowers,

Asylumed beneath arms create to bless,
    And surely shield with sky-appointed powers;
Each thread of yellow hair numbered, for aye,
    Each lisp of childish love construed to tune,
While patient eyes behold the bud of May
    Ripen and burst into the flower of June.


But th' cold black earth is strewn with lily-leaves,
    The air with spoils of fern,
And one rejoiced, but now one sorely grieves,
    And many grieve, in turn;
Alas, the wasted flowers dislimbed and lorn,
    Their scented hope and fair ambition slain,
Alas, the virgin blooms tear-wrung and torn,
    That seek asylum on the homeless plain.


Ah, well a day, where are the tears of men,
    Where Pity's dwelling-place—
Do these that bleed invoke them less than when
    Pink smiles are on their face?
O, hard, cold eyes, that have no gentle spark
    That may relent a little and be kind,
Is there no mercy-ray can pierce their dark,
    No tender light to show them they are blind?
Howbeit, the flowers are wasted with fierce woe,
    Fair leaves are cast apart,
And Beauty's feet leave red stains as they go,
    Leave cries as from the heart!


Shame! that Earth's beauteous tendrils should be born
    To the dread fate of early wanton blight;
Shame! that the rosy blush of youthful Morn
Should hide beneath the craggy brows of Night . .

Oh! Night! reign thou, when goddess Strength doth reign,
   And Weakness cries unto the blind, deaf Sea,
When tender Innocence doth plead in vain
   But for the grateful privilege—to be!

Poor, ruined blossoms of the green, glad Spring,
   Brought premature to Winter's bitter end,
Lo! Death shall be your last remorseless sting,
   And Heaven prove your first reposeful friend.

\*   \*   \*   \*   \*   \*   \*   \*

But doubt not that who despoil these flowers,
   Shall take, anon, a keen, swift tooth to heart,
That shall cut through the comfort of his hours,
   And cause their dry, dead blood to fright and start,
And tremble, pale and red upon the brow . .
   Yea, Night shall cover him right thankfully,
Until he learn the mightiness to bow
   Before the righteous Love he did deny.

## "WHERE ROLLS THE OREGON"

> "Or lose thyself in the continuous woods
> Where rolls the Oregon, and hears no sound
> Save his own dashings—yet the dead are there
> \* \* \* The dead reign there alone."
> 
> BRYANT.

Pine scented vales and verdure-mantled hills,
And sweet the air where rolls the Oregon!

The dead no longer reign alone! they came
And went, the Aztec and his brother red,
Nor in the chartless woods left other trace
Than dust of a yellow flower's fading bloom!
But white Sierra's deathless walls remain,
And icy spires the sky's blue vesture breaks,
Sublime and still where rolls the Oregon!

Mother of men! O, save thy later born!
A race complexioned like thy mountain brows,
And sinewed like thy rocky hills salutes thee!
Above the dashings of the resolute sea
A new sound stirs; the roar of busy wheels
Acclaims its conquest where the dead speak not,
And the bronze anvil with heroic ring,
Doth melodise the breath of human life.
The dead are dead! but o'er the common grave,
Proud Time has swept with singing pinion,

And from gray dust a golden grain beams back
The glory of the sun, and milky corn
Waves o'er the ashes of the past. Afar,
Ripe orchards bow with purple pulp, and 'mid
The vine-clad slopes, and by tralucent streams
That chant soft monodies of peace, the grazing
Herd meanders, and reposeful hamlets,
Sleek with the thrift of fortunate stars,
Lie nested in the lap of odorous pines.

———————

Lo! here the men of forty-nine have come!
A new lord, now, with yon stark skeleton
Disputes the empire of the West! the land
Of roseate glades where rolls the Oregon!

## YOSEMITE

O, eloquent Earth! this thing hath delighted thy face,
Here where the great rocks have blossomed in passion of grace
Here where the mountains were cleft by the tread of the snow,
The light of their crowns re-gemmed in the lakelets below:
The torrent that carved out the hills with its furious flare,
As the veil of a bride now sways in the tremulous air,
As the trail of a ribbon now glints o'er yon tolerant plain,
That smiles in song of th' sun and swells to th' kiss of the rain,
Yea, conflict of fire-gods hath ruptured the rocks in a night,
And mountains fell and arose by shock of the fire-king's might,
And domes of a temple of God of all gods did arise,
To fill all the spaces with praise from the seas to the skies.

## LYRIC OF LABOR

**UPHARSIN IS WRIT ON THE WALL!**

Let us raise up a tocsin of warning,
   We that toil on the shore and the sea,
Our song is the song of the morning,
   And our theme is the right to be free;
The light of the sky has been breaking,
   We have seen what the clouds had in thrall,
The tyrants that held us are quaking,
   For Upharsin is writ on the wall!

We toil but we do not inherit,
   We build but we do not possess,
The flower of our skill and our merit
   Only blossoms for others to bless,
It is time that Right cried a warning,
   That Justice had thundered her call:
Our song is the song of the morning,
   And Upharsin is writ on the wall!

Sweet freedom is ours if we dare it,
   Demand it with resolute will,
And the gold that we coin we shall share it,
   The fruit of the forge and the mill;
The creators of wealth cry a warning,
   A new hope shines forth for us all:
Our song is the song of the morning,
   And Upharsin is writ on the wall!

# A TRINODY

ABELARD AND HELOISE
ANTONY AND CLEOPATRA
PAOLO AND FRANCESCA

# A TRINODY

## ABELARD AND HELOISE

### ABELARD

"Forget to love! and lose the love of thee!
Not while remains a sense or sign of me;
Not for the boon that Christ is said to give,
Not without thee the days of heaven to live . .
Ah, if I could I'd love thee something less;
The fear that I may lose thee brings distress,
And ofttimes sickens at my sick heart's roots,
And teaches pain the lightning of its shoots . . .
Lose thee! thy lips, love, life, thy magic touch!
The worship that I pray and plead so much,
Thy fairy feet that climb about my heart,
Thy roseate form that mocks the trace of art,
Rather, high God, I would I had not been,
Or who should slay me would commit no sin . . .
Thy subtle love has searched my utmost life,
And made thy soul my soul's immortal wife,
Until whate'er of rapture fans my flame
Is needs familiar with thy sense and name;
The sun less warm than thy benign embrace,
Music less sweet than language of thy face,
Nor any flower's white, glowing, silken nest,
Can plead the sweet and softness of thy breast;
All sweets of earth 't were idle court to crave,
For in the gift of thee all sweets I have!"

## HELOISE

" What thing shall dare to measure what thou art?
Love has made thee oceans to my heart,
And marked thee with the juices of quick wine,
And filled the heavens with thy life and mine!
But if thou go'st away where will I go,
Where will my passion rend its tortured throe?
Ah! Love has made for thee a place to dwell,
More quick with life than earth or heaven or hell,
And taught thy touch more witcheries of sense
Than Summer knows with all her vigilance;
I do not fear that thou wilt hie away,
I am too much a parcel of thy day;
Have stolen through and slept in all thy veins,
And mingled with the sources of thy pains,
Toyed with thy love-thougths as with silken curls,
Seeing they bore the faces of glad girls,
And oh! so far in thy life's temple stole,
That I have grown a portion of thy soul!"

# ANTONY AND CLEOPATRA

### ANTONY

I saw light burning on a woman's face!
And chafing 'neath my life besought the place,
Nor asked if 'twas the sign of Death or Love—
Gift of Osiris or our father Jove—
That, magnet like, attracted with fine heat,
'Till I did yield, kissing the flames' soft feet!
"Pour all thy vials, love, poisons or wines,
If the sharp vintage of thy purple vines,
Charged by the frenzied alchemy of bliss,
Drown me in the heavenly abyss!
The mad excess of life—excess of thee!
The meshes and the measures of infinity!"

### CLEOPATRA

"Ah! Love has sprinkled thee with such delight
My languid eyes are lost to other sight. .
Now as I see thee my exultant breast—
In softer hours oft thy Lethean nest—
Swelling doth welcome thee; all my soul aches
For thee, joys in thee, welcomes thee, and takes
The familiar channels that conduct to thee
And the ripe board of heavenly agony. . .

Sigh yet again, sweet lord! I feel thy breath
As the warm stories of a summer heath
Whispered to mine: my veins are full and thine,
Our lips do homage at a common shrine,
The while the distilled honey of thy sighs—
Soul-sighs more holy sweet than paradise—
Impregnates like a poison all my life,
The glow of love and passion of its strife!"

A TRINODY

# PAOLO AND FRANCESCA

### PAOLO

In summer dreams I found a new delight,
And stung by it as beauty stings the sight,
Fell to it worshiping . . . all younger signs
Of light and flowers and golden rooted wines,
Smells of amorous spring and sins of sense.
Cleaving apart from the omnipotence !
I felt the first born breath of passion's strife,
The traces of soft feet upon my life,
And touches of the palpitating stir
Of liquid sighs and seasons goodlier
Than throes of music melting on the wing,
Or the wild morn when bliss first knew her sting !
From the sweet meshes of the perfect hour,
One whose precious sex was her first power,
Drew nigh, crowding the sight with loveliness,
And my rapt being with a sweet distress:
Oh, fate! may I but touch whereon she's trod!
Thus touching an abundance of good God,
Or live th' insane existence of a kiss!
Or die because of wild excess of bliss!

Feasting this joy with my enhungered gaze,
Exhausted sight grew vocal in her praise,

And keen desire's young and luxurious spur,
Dared the approach my being made to her:
" Whence came—if thither thou wilt not repair—
Creature of light and love, I have no care:
Perchance thy birthright is some warm white star,
Or tender scented foam flowers that are
The joys of voluptuous bosomed sea!
Whate'er thou art a heaven art thou to me,
And from this hour my life my heaven or hell,
Or sweet oblivion that shall drown this spell!
O, let me bask in thy dear witchery,
Approach thee close, this wise, and worship thee
Beneath th' electric fervor of thy touch,
For sweet Elysium cannot bless so much:
Thy person wears the smell of many flowers;
Thy moments are the essence of great hours . .
Would I could die entangled in thy toils,
Surer to save than Nazareth's sweated spoils,
Finding contentment—if thou diest too—
And bear the burden of thy blisses through."

Like the intense wooing by the great gold sun
Of a pink moss rose I wooed and won . .
Obtained the treasury of a look from her,
A pause that was the sublimest minister
That e'er converted to idolatry:
And pausing she did hear my tell-tale sigh,
That labored deep as shell-loves of the sea,
Or girl-loves in their young intensity;
And read the frenzied speeches of great eyes,
Fed by her charms as by a paradise,
And knew they were the stories of love's lyre,
The syllables of rapture and desire!

## FRANCESCA

" Thou hast awaked me from a barren dream,
And wild emotions taught me for a theme !
O, Life ! O, lovely contemplation mine,
I see the years flow on like purple wine,
The happy, happy years, create by thee,
Filled with our glad, our dual destiny ! . .
Aye, for this life to which thou art the door,
Which life thou art thyself with its sweet lore,
I wed thee to my very inmost heart,
And wear thee as my being's warmest part . .
O, what a glorious thing art thou strange lord,
What new delights thy wondrous words afford :
I'd melt with tears the stony-hearted powers,
Were there an end to thy love freighted hours,
Were there a period to the toils that yearn,
Or time when thy soft breathing would not burn !
O, great sweet Lord, bless thou my lord and I,
At this proud birth of our eternity ! "

# THE BIRTH OF SONG

# The Birth of Song

## I

Out of the voiceless years,
And bitter seasons of the days of men,
A sudden wondrous thing pipes into ears
Untried till now of sweet or joy . . as when
The morning stars poured forth their roundelays
    At th' birth-time of strange days.

## II

And glad are they that hear . .
The first that listed to the faint first tune
That broke from Silence with a vivid cheer,
The breath of Maia and the voice of June,
Wreathed into flowers of living harmony,
    Afloat from sea to sky.

## III

Joy that the mute shall speak . .
The dumb, dead, barren Earth, arise voice-given,
To join the planet-chorus with fierce shriek
Of new delight, as it were born of heaven—
Yea, the fair gods rejoice when one is born
    With song from out the morn!

## IV

    Joy that the dead have life—
That waste, torn, bitter shreds of clay take form,
And blush in travail of a fruitful strife,
The law of calm, the method of the storm,
Fair token of a Future big with fate,
    And Man's soul-warmed estate.

## V

    When the great sea shall pause,
And hie within herself with modest mien;
Nor with loud lungs proclaim the strength that was
Above the use that is . . and she is seen
In ways of gentler grace and calmer power,
    As she were near her hour—

## VI

    The Venus-birth of Love—
With the wide East afire with gold and white,
And sweet warm atmospheres deep interwove
With rosy boys and flowers of crimson light,
And vocal with the sweet, slight song that she
    Hath conjured from the sea!

## VII

    And sound hath found new voice—
The mermaid choir, the sirens of the shore,
With softer-throated rhetoric rejoice,
Where Ocean rude affrighted with his roar,
And fierce curled tongues found no sweet word to say
    In the dread round of day.

## VIII

And man who had come forth
Flowering upon the hills like leaves of spring,
Stood still as he had stood not on the earth,
Hearing a strange fair swan in God's name sing,
Tender and low yet vivid with sweet might,
    As it were vocal light!

## IX

Stood still as very death..
Awe-stricken with this thing that Time began..
For sound had not essayed with gentler breath
Than the beast's growl or growl of beastly man!
But now he spake when ceased the silver rune
    With voice soft like the tune!

## X

And in his valiant eye—
Whose fire was from the angry lightning caught.
Whose only culture ere the beast should die,
To gaze into his burning eye-balls, fraught
With rage and hell and death withouten fear—
    There now stood forth a tear!

## XI

A sight to marvel at
Where brows were woven hard in a steel woof
With Night for shuttle; the stout web begat
Where cold and tempest interwed aloof,
Afore the fountains of the soul took form,
    Sparkling from out the storm.

## XII

Or where men toiled, forsooth,
And wrestled wretchedly in harsh stern ways,
This sweet stole forth the venom of Toil's tooth,
And merry made the heart of heavy days,
As from the curtain of the radiant sky,
    Quick colors kissed the eye!

## XIII

Yea, God wot, some sweet thing,
Hath tamed the dark, dire temper fetched from hell,
And where the scepter stormed a gentle string,
Pours trembling forth its overweening spell,
Caught of some sounds the sweet God's breath did leaven
    Deep in the throat of heaven.

## XIV

And no brass chain like this,
The panther's lair can hold hard fast and true,
Or make the leopard's eye the thing to kiss,
Or Lea's neck the place where pleasure grew,
As in the meshes of his mighty curls,
    There nested blue-eyed girls!

## XV

For now a new sense came,
And hearing was there where none heard before;
Fair heaven's arch resounded with a flame,
That awed earth with its palpitating lore,
The voice of Israfil or Syrinx reed,
    That erst no ear gave heed.

## XVI

Yea, now, the great god Pan,
From his split hoof of clay to th' celestial brow,
Radiant with stars and suns is known to man;
Yea, now, his seven wondrous spells aglow,
Streamed from the singing bosoms of the skies,
    Blending in sweet surprise.

## XVII

Thus had th' immortal gods,
Been filled and feasted with harmonious wine,
New ears now list the soul-entrancing rods,
The later god invokes the heavenly Nine,
And to Olympus linked hymns deep and long—
    The worship born of song!

## XVIII

And to the leaping strain,
Forth from the joyous vale and jocund wood,
With Ceres and the Vine-god in the train,
Dance the delighted nymphs in rosy mood;
Camilla's feet not lighter sped the corn,
    Than these from morn to morn.

## XIX

All Nature fair rejoiced,
With quick fecundity through all her veins;
The feathered tribes a-chorus happy-voiced,
Atuned their eager nestlings to the strains,
The sheep's lean dugs with fresh milk filled anew,
    Glad'ning the shepherd's view.

## XX

And lo! in Illus' land,
Some hardy men a city well desired,
That laughing scorned the toil of each vain hand:
But now the dead stones moved as they were fired.
By some God's breath, and each in lusty chase,
    Climbed, singing, to his place

## XXI

With light ecstatic bound;
Nor with rude fronts with unshorn locks afright,
But smooth and fair Dardanus rose, and round,
Glad wing-ed walls encompassed her with might,
And men rejoiced in her—wrought free of hire—
    Sweet labor of the lyre!

## XXII

Hark, now, upon the air,
"Io Pæan" deep in the East's bright lap,
Acclaimed from lusty throats, or brown or fair,
And "Io," lordlier still, as o'er the gap,
Beside bright Hesper Phœbus blushed away..
    "Io" throughout the day!

## XXIII

And to the night's breath given,
Impassioned with loud unisons that move
The star courts of propitiating heaven..
Until responsive to the hymn of love,
The god's celestial sister with soft zest
    Beams melodies of rest.

## XXIV

And thou art wise, thou Song,
The dangers of the deep of sin are passed
With thy transporting compass swift and strong,
Each gold-lipped siren unto silence cast,
Outsung by one that conquereth the sea—
    More eloquent than she!

## XXV

And to the Orphic strain
The serpent basked a-listening; the roar
Of the free beast was hushed as Vesta's fane;
And as Apollo's son twixt either shore
Winged his ecstatic lyre, the leafy wood,
    Enamored of the mood,

## XXVI

Moved headlong with smooth stride;
And the pliant streams their laggard beds o'erstepped
To follow the meandering limpid tide
Of tune, as musical as he that crept
From Pæan, vanquished, Marsyas of old,
    Babbling o'er keys of gold!

## XXVII

Or in the nether hell,
Lo, the untried miracle of music sweet!
Imprisoning the prison by his spell,
Till all the place lay prone beside his feet,
Till the will of ebony-crowned Dis was made
    The will of him that played!

## XXVIII

Till all forgot their pains,
And mocking labors of untiring woe,
Typhœus' burthens or Ægean's chains,
And Eurydice with sweet leave to go,
Fired with fierce hope pursued the strain of fire—
  Glad victory of the lyre!

## XXIX

And so pursued all men
The stream that bore the wing-ed fruit of song!
By the mirthful shore of vocal Helicon,
Where Philomela poured her flood along,
To Amphion's song-built Thebes where Memnon's
  The bright dawn made rejoice!

## XXX

And for song's highest reach,
One was awakened on Parnassus' side,
To sing of Troy o'er all the lords of speech!
The Nine gave him the harp to Thamyras denied,
And he to Earth the key to harmony—
  To tune its voices by.